Song of the Morning

We are an Easter people

and 'ALLELUIA' is our song.

ST AUGUSTINE

Song of the Morning

Easter Stories and Poems for Children

A Special Collection
compiled by Pat Alexander

Illustrated by Robin Lawrie

Published by
Lion Publishing plc
Sandy Lane West, Oxford, England
ISBN 0 7459 3209 6
Lion Publishing
4050 Lee Vance View, Colorado Springs, CO 80918, USA
ISBN 0 7459 3742 X
Albatross Books Pty Ltd
PO Box 320, Sutherland, NSW 2232, Australia
ISBN 0 7324 1223 4

First edition 1997
10 9 8 7 6 5 4 3 2 1 0

A catalogue record for this book is available
from the British Library

Printed and bound in Spain

Contents

8 'It's All Right!' 149

9 A New Beginning 169

About This Book

Easter eggs, chocolate bunnies – what do we really celebrate at Easter? Is it the return of spring? In the countries of the northern hemisphere, Easter does come in the springtime. But half the world has Easter in the fall. So there must be more to it than golden daffodils and fat, bursting buds.

And of course there is! The Easter festival celebrates the death and rising to life of Jesus – events that lie at the heart of the Christian faith. Christians, in the words of St Augustine, 'are an Easter people'. Everything they believe and hope for springs out of the Easter events. That's why they are still celebrating, 2000 years on. And the world joins in, because there's nothing like a good celebration!

The stories and poems in this book explore and reflect on God's rescue plan, from the very beginning when things went so badly wrong to Good Friday and Easter Day. Many of them draw on the great Easter themes of costly love, of quarrels mended, wrongs forgiven, and the new beginnings that this makes possible. If that sounds rather serious, you will find plenty of fun on the way. I've even included a clutch of 'Eggs for Easter' for you to find.

I have really enjoyed discovering and choosing these stories and poems. I hope you will enjoy them too. If you would like to write and tell me about it, you can send your letters to Lion Publishing (the address is on page 4), and they will make sure I get them.

Until then, good reading. And a happy Easter!

PAT ALEXANDER
Iffley, Oxford, 1997

1
How Things Began

Easter is the exciting climax to a story that began long, long before. To understand it we must go back to the very beginning – to the Bible's own story of how things began. That is retold in my first story, *The Good and the Bad*. Bob Hartman's two stories tell it in a slightly different way, for younger readers.

C.S. Lewis takes us to a different world – the land of Narnia. *The Magician's Nephew* tells how it was called into being. But Narnia, like our own world, was soon spoiled. And in *The Lion, the Witch and the Wardrobe* the whole land lies under the power of the White Witch.

The Good and the Bad

From *The Lion Children's Bible*

PAT ALEXANDER

This story comes from the first book of the Bible, Genesis, chapters 1–3.

Long ago, when things began, God made our world. He made the sun to light the day. He made the moon and stars for the night. He made the sky and land and sea.

He made birds to fly in the sky, fish to swim in the sea, and animals for the land. God looked around at all that he had made, and he was pleased. It was very good. The world was ready for people. So God made a man and a woman – Adam and Eve.

God put Adam and Eve in charge of his new world – to look after the plants and trees, the birds and fish and animals. He gave them a lovely place to live in. There were cool rivers, shady trees, and all kinds of fruit to eat. The place was called the garden of Eden.

Adam and Eve were very happy. There was just one thing that God told them they must never do. They were not to eat the fruit of one special tree – the tree of the knowledge of good and evil. If they did, God said they would die. So Adam and Eve lived as God's friends. And did as he said.

But there was someone who wanted to spoil God's world. One day, as Eve was walking past the special tree – the tree of the knowledge of good and evil – she heard the soft, hissing voice of the snake.

'See how good this fruit is. Doesn't it make your mouth water? Why not try it? The fruit will make you wise. If you eat it you will be as clever as God is.'

Eve listened to the snake's soft voice. She looked at the fruit. And she forgot how good and kind God was. She wanted to be as clever as God. She wanted to do as she liked.

Eve stretched out her hand and picked the fruit. She began to eat – and she gave some to Adam.

From that moment things began to go wrong.

God knew what Adam and Eve had done. No one can hide anything from him. Adam and Eve weren't God's friends any more, and he sent them away.

They had to leave the garden of Eden, where they had been so happy, where they had walked and talked with God. An angel with a sword stood guard to stop them ever coming back.

Now they had to work hard, so hard that they ached with tiredness. They learned what pain felt like. But worst of all, God's dreadful warning came true; they knew that when they grew old, they would die.

God's new world, the world that was so good, was already spoiled.

'In the Beginning'

STEVE TURNER

God said WORLD
and the world spun round,
God said LIGHT
and the light beamed down,
God said LAND
and the sea rolled back,
God said NIGHT
and the sky went black.

God said LEAF
and the shoot pushed through,
God said FIN
and the first fish grew,
God said BEAK
and the big bird soared,
God said FUR
and the jungle roared.

God said SKIN
and the man breathed air,
God said BONE
and the girl stood there.
God said GOOD
and the world was great.
God said REST
and they all slept late.

'This is Good!'

From *The Lion Storyteller Bible*

BOB HARTMAN

At first, there wasn't anything at all. Nothing! So God set to work. But he didn't use his hands, or a special machine. He spoke, that's all. He said, 'I'd like some light.' And there was light. Brighter than a summer morning or a thousand Christmas candles.

God spoke again. He said, 'Sky. I'd like some sky. And some water underneath.' And, sure enough, there it was. The bright blue sky. With the dark blue heavens above it. And the blue-green sea below.

'Earth.' That's what God said next, hard and firm, as if he really meant it. And the blue-green waters parted, and there was dry land underneath. Great patches of it, dirt black and brown. Here and there, all over the world.

'We need some colour,' God whispered, as if he were thinking out loud. And, quivering with excitement, green growing things crept right up out of the dark earth, then burst into blossom – red, orange and blue! Pine trees and palm trees. Rose bushes and blackberry bushes. Tulips and chrysanthemums.

God shouted next.

'Day – shining sun!'

'Night – shining moon!'

'Bright shining stars!'

And there they were, for morning and evening, summer and winter – time and heat and light!

After that, God called to the sky, as if he were expecting some kind of an answer.

'Come forth, flying things!' he called.

And through the clouds they came. Flying high and flying low. Flying large and flying small. Eagles and insects. Hummingbirds and hawks.

Then God called to the sea.

'Come forth, splashing things!'

And they came to him, too, leaping right up through the waves.

Sailfish and swordfish. Dolphins and trout. Great grinning humpbacked whales.

Finally, God called to the earth.

'Come forth, walking things, crawling things, running, hopping, climbing things!'

And sure enough, they came. Up from burrows. Down from trees. Out of the high grass, and across the open plains.

Now everything was ready. Good and ready. So God spoke again.

'Man and woman,' is what he said, as if he were calling the names of his very best friends.

And out of the dust came Adam and Eve. To enjoy all that God had made. To take care of it for him. And to talk with him.

'This is the way things ought to be,' God said at last. 'This is good!'

The Founding of Narnia

From *The Magician's Nephew*

C.S. LEWIS

Narnia is the realm of Aslan the Lion – and The Magician's Nephew *is the book that tells how 'all the comings and goings between our world and the land of Narnia first began'. Thanks to cunning Uncle Andrew and his magic rings, Polly and Digory find themselves in another world. At first everything is dark. And then the song begins – a song that calls stars and planets into being. In the eastern sky a sun appears, and at last they can see the Singer: a huge and shaggy Lion…*

The Lion was pacing to and fro about that empty land and singing his new song. It was softer and more lilting than the song by which he had called up the stars and the sun; a gentle, rippling music. And as he walked and sang the valley grew green with grass. It spread out from the Lion like a pool. It ran up the sides of the little hills like a wave. In a few minutes it was creeping up the lower slopes of the distant mountains, making that young world every moment softer. The light wind could now be heard ruffling the grass. Soon there were other things besides grass. The higher slopes grew dark with heather. Patches of rougher and more bristling green appeared in the valley. Digory did not know what they were until one began coming up quite close to him. It was a little, spiky thing that threw out dozens of arms and covered these arms with green and grew larger at the rate of about an inch every two seconds. There were dozens of these things all round him now. When they were nearly as tall as himself he saw what they were. 'Trees!' he exclaimed…

All this time the Lion's song, and his stately prowl, to and fro, backwards and forwards, was going on…

Polly was finding the song more and more interesting because she thought she was beginning to see the connection between the music and the things that were happening. When a line of dark firs sprang up on a ridge about a hundred yards away she felt that they were connected with a series of deep, prolonged notes which the Lion had sung a second before. And when he burst into a rapid series of lighter notes she was not surprised to see primroses suddenly appearing in every direction. Thus, with an unspeakable thrill, she felt quite certain that all the things were coming (as she said) 'out of the Lion's head'. When you listened to his song you heard the things he was making up: when you looked round you, you saw them...

The Lion was singing still. But now the song had once more changed. It was more like what we should call a tune, but it was also far wilder. It made you want to run and jump and climb. It made you want to shout.

Can you imagine a stretch of grassy land bubbling like water in a pot? For that is really the best description of what was happening. In all directions it was swelling into humps. They were of very different sizes, some no bigger than mole-hills, some as big as wheel-barrows, two the size of cottages. And the humps moved and swelled till they burst, and the crumbled earth poured out of them, and from each hump there came out an animal... The dogs came out, barking the moment their heads were free, and struggling as you've seen them do when they are getting through a narrow hole in a hedge. The stags were the queerest to watch, for of course the antlers came up a long time before the rest of them, so at first Digory thought they were trees. The frogs, who all came up near the river, went straight into it with a plop-plop and a loud croaking. The panthers, leopards and things of that sort, sat down at once to wash the loose earth off their hind quarters and then stood up against the trees to sharpen their front claws. Showers of birds came out of the trees. Butterflies fluttered. Bees got to work on the flowers as if they hadn't a second to lose. But the greatest moment of all was when the biggest hump broke like a small earthquake and out came the sloping back, the large, wise head, and the four baggy-trousered legs of an elephant. And now you could hardly hear the song of the Lion; there was so much cawing, cooing, crowing, braying, neighing, baying, barking, lowing, bleating, and trumpeting...

And now, for the first time, the Lion was quite silent. He was going to and fro among the animals. And every now and then he would go up to two of them (always two at a time) and touch their noses with his. He would touch two beavers among all the beavers, two leopards among all the leopards, one stag and one deer among all the deer, and leave the rest. Some sorts of animal he passed over altogether. But the pairs which he had touched instantly left their own kinds and followed him. At last he stood still and all the creatures whom he had touched came and stood in a wide circle around him. The others whom he had not touched began to wander away. Their noises faded gradually into the distance. The chosen beasts who remained were now utterly silent, all with their eyes fixed intently upon the Lion. The cat-like ones gave an occasional twitch of the tail but otherwise all were still...

The Lion, whose eyes never blinked, stared at the animals as hard as if he was going to burn them up with his mere stare. And gradually a change came over them. The smaller ones – the rabbits, moles and such-like – grew a good deal larger. The very big ones – you noticed it most with the elephants – grew a little smaller. Many animals sat up on their hind legs. Most put their heads on one side as if they were trying very hard to understand. The Lion opened his mouth, but no sound came from it; he was breathing out, a long, warm breath; it seemed to sway all the beasts as the wind sways a line of trees. Far overhead from beyond the veil of blue sky which hid them the stars sang again: a pure, cold, difficult music. Then there came a swift flash like fire (but it burnt nobody) either from the sky or from the Lion itself, and every drop of blood tingled in the children's bodies, and the deepest, wildest voice they had ever heard was saying: 'Narnia, Narnia, Narnia, awake. Love. Think. Speak. Be walking trees. Be talking beasts.'

A Sad Day

From *The Lion Storyteller Bible*

BOB HARTMAN

'Welcome to my world!' God said to Adam. 'It's good, isn't it?'

'Welcome to my garden!' God said to Eve. 'This is the most beautiful place of all. And I want it to be your home. Take care of the animals for me. Take care of the plants. And eat whatever you like. There are plenty of trees to pick from.'

Adam and Eve didn't know what to say. They looked at the garden. They looked at each other. And then they smiled the world's first smile.

Life was going to be perfect here. Just perfect.

'There's just one more thing,' God said. 'Do you see that tree over there? The one in the middle of the garden? Well, the fruit on that tree is not good for you. If you eat it, you will make me very unhappy. And you will have to leave this beautiful place.'

Adam and Eve looked at each other again. With so many trees to choose from, that hardly seemed to be a problem. And for a long time, they were content with soft juicy pears, sweet thick-skinned oranges, and round ripe melons.

Then, one day, the serpent came to visit.

'Tell me,' the serpent said to Eve, 'which trees are you allowed to eat from?'

'Every tree!' Eve smiled. 'Except the one in the middle of the garden.'

'Oh?' said the crafty serpent. 'And why is that?'

'Because it would make God unhappy,' Eve answered. 'And we would have to leave this beautiful place.'

'Ridiculous!' laughed the serpent. 'God does not want you to eat that fruit because he knows it would make you as clever as him. You know all about being good. But God has told you nothing about what it means to be bad. Eat the fruit, and you will know all about that, too!'

Eve thought that the fruit looked delicious. She had sometimes wondered what it tasted like. And it wasn't really fair of God to keep things from them.

So she picked a piece. And took a bite. And gave Adam a taste as well.

And, right away, they discovered what it meant to do something bad. Their stomachs churned with guilt. Their faces turned red with shame. And instead of running to meet God when he next visited the garden, they ran away to hide.

'I know what you have done,' God called out sadly. 'Now you will have to leave this beautiful place.'

'Goodbye,' God said to Adam. 'From now on, you will have to scratch at the earth for the food you eat.'

'Goodbye,' God said to Eve. 'Your life will be hard, too.'

'And when your lives end,' God said finally, 'you will go back to the ground from which you came.'

Adam and Eve looked at each other. Then they walked sadly out of the garden. They had learned what it means to be bad. And they had changed God's good world for ever.

'There is a smudge of bad in all of us'

MICHAEL DUGGAN (AGED 12)

There is a smudge of bad in all of us,
Something that is there deep inside,
Nagging a space for itself,
Something that can't be dug out with a spade,
Knocked out with a hammer,
Threatened out with fire.
But it's there
And it flavours whatever we do.

The White Witch

From *The Lion, the Witch and the Wardrobe*

C.S. LEWIS

The Witch got into Narnia by accident, at the very beginning, with Polly and Digory and Uncle Andrew. When this story begins, Aslan the Lion has been away a long time, and the White Witch has brought cruel winter to the land. Lucy has found her way into Narnia through the wardrobe and met Mr Tumnus the Faun and some of the creatures. Now her brother Edmund has followed. But he is stopped by a beautiful lady all wrapped in white fur, who arrives on a sledge drawn by reindeer and driven by a fat dwarf…

'Stop!' said the Lady, and the dwarf pulled the reindeer up so sharp that they almost sat down. Then they recovered themselves and stood champing their bits and blowing. In the frosty air the breath coming out of their nostrils looked like smoke.

'And what, pray, are you?' said the Lady, looking hard at Edmund.

'I'm – I'm – my name's Edmund,' said Edmund rather awkwardly. He did not like the way she looked at him.

The Lady frowned. 'Is that how you address a Queen?' she asked, looking sterner than ever.

'I beg your pardon, your Majesty, I didn't know,' said Edmund.

'Not know the Queen of Narnia?' cried she. 'Ha! You shall know us better hereafter. But I repeat – what are you?… Are you a great overgrown dwarf that has cut off its beard?'

'No, your Majesty,' said Edmund, 'I never had a beard, I'm a boy.'

'A boy!' said she. 'Do you mean you are a Son of Adam?… Are you human?'

'Yes, your Majesty,' said Edmund.

'And how, pray, did you come to enter my dominions?'

'Please, your Majesty, I came in through a wardrobe.'

'A wardrobe? What do you mean?'

'I – I opened a door and just found myself here, your Majesty,' said Edmund.

'Ha!' said the Queen, speaking more to herself than to him. 'A door. A door from the world of men! I have heard of such things. This may wreck all. But he is only one, and he is easily dealt with.' As she spoke these words she rose from her seat and looked Edmund full in the face, her eyes flaming; at the same moment she raised her wand. Edmund felt sure that she was going to do something dreadful but he seemed unable to move. Then, just as he gave himself up for lost, she appeared to change her mind.

'My poor child,' she said in quite a different voice, 'how cold you look! Come and sit with me here on the sledge and I will put my mantle round you and we will talk.'

Edmund did not like this arrangement at all but he dared not disobey; he stepped on to the sledge and sat at her feet, and she put a fold of her fur mantle around him and tucked it well in.

'Perhaps something hot to drink?' said the Queen. 'Should you like that?... What would you like best to eat?'

'Turkish Delight, please, your Majesty,' said Edmund.

The Queen let another drop fall from her bottle on to the snow, and instantly there appeared a round box, tied with green silk ribbon, which, when opened, turned out to contain several pounds of the best Turkish Delight. Each piece was sweet and light to the very centre and Edmund had never tasted anything more delicious. He was quite warm now, and very comfortable.

While he was eating the Queen kept asking him questions. At first Edmund tried to remember that it is rude to speak with one's mouth full, but soon he forgot about this and thought only of trying to shovel down as much Turkish Delight as he could, and the more he ate the more he wanted to eat, and he never asked himself why the Queen should be so inquisitive. She got him to tell her that he had one brother and two sisters, and that one of his sisters had already been to Narnia and had met a Faun there, and that no one except himself and his brother and his sisters knew anything about Narnia...

At last the Turkish Delight was all finished and Edmund was looking very hard at the empty box and wishing that she would ask him whether he would like some more. Probably the Queen knew quite well what he was thinking; for she knew, though Edmund did not, that this was enchanted Turkish Delight and that anyone who had once tasted it would want more and more of it... But she did not offer him any more. Instead, she said to him, 'Son of Adam, I should so much like to see your brother and your two sisters. Will you bring them to see me?... Because, if you did come again – bringing them with you of course – I'd be able to give you some more Turkish Delight.'

'Please, please,' said Edmund... 'couldn't I have just one piece of Turkish Delight to eat on the way home?'

'No, no,' said the Queen with a laugh, 'you must wait till next time.' While she spoke, she signalled to the dwarf to drive on, but as the sledge swept away out of sight, the Queen waved to Edmund, calling out, 'Next time! Next time! Don't forget. Come soon.'

Edmund was still staring after the sledge when he heard someone calling his own name, and looking round he saw Lucy coming towards him from another part of the wood.

'Oh, Edmund!' she cried. 'So you've got in too!... If I'd known you had got in I'd have waited for you... I've been having lunch with dear Mr Tumnus, the Faun, and he's very well, and the White Witch has done nothing to him...'

'The White Witch?' said Edmund; 'who's she?'

'She is a perfectly terrible person,' said Lucy. 'She calls herself the Queen of Narnia though she has no right to be queen at all, and all the Fauns and Dryads and Naiads and Dwarfs and Animals – at least all the good ones – simply hate her. And she can turn people into stone and do all kinds of horrible things. And she has made a magic so that it is always winter in Narnia – always winter, but it never gets to Christmas. And she drives about on a sledge, drawn by reindeer, with her wand in her hand and a crown on her head.'

Edmund was already feeling uncomfortable from having eaten too many sweets, and when he heard that the Lady he had made friends with was a dangerous witch he felt even more uncomfortable. But he still wanted to taste that Turkish Delight again more than he wanted anything else.

'Who told you all that stuff about the White Witch?' he asked.

'Mr Tumnus, the Faun,' said Lucy.

'You can't always believe what Fauns say,' said Edmund...

2
The Rescue Plan

Once badness was let loose in our world it got everywhere. It got into everything and everyone: 'a smudge of bad in all of us' as Michael Duggan's poem puts it. The world had become a sad, dark place. But God never stopped loving his world and everyone in it. He wanted make it light again. And God had a rescue plan – a rescue person – to deal with the badness once and for all…

A Light in the Dark

From 'The Christmas Story' in *The Manger is Empty*

WALTER WANGERIN

Once upon a time the world was dark, and the land where the people lived was deep in darkness. It was as dark as the night in the daytime. It had been dark for so long that the people had forgotten what the light was like. This is what they did: they lit small candles for themselves and pretended it was day. But the world was a gloomy place, and the people who walked in darkness were lonelier than they knew, and the lonely people were sadder than they could say.

But God was in love with the world.

God looked down from heaven and saw that the earth was stuck, like a clock, at midnight. 'No,' he said. 'This isn't good. It's time to make time tick again. Time, time,' said the mighty God, 'to turn the earth from night to morning.'

And God was in love with the people especially.

He saw their little candlelight, and he pitied their pretending. 'They think they see,' he said, 'but all they see is shadow, and people are frightened by shadows. Poor people!' he said. 'They wonder why they are afraid.' God watched the people move about like fireflies in the night, and he shook his head. 'Poor people, pretending to be happy,' he said. 'Well, I want them to be happy. It's time,' declared the Lord our God. 'It's time to do a new thing! I'll shatter their darkness. I will send the sunlight down so they can see and know that they are seeing!'

God so loved the world, that he sent his only son into the world itself.

The King Born in a Stable

From *The Lion Children's Bible*

PAT ALEXANDER

This story comes from the New Testament. You can read it in Matthew's Gospel, chapter 1, and Luke's Gospel, chapter 2.

Joseph the carpenter was worried. Mary, the girl he loved, was expecting a baby. It wasn't his baby; and they weren't married. The gossip had started already. He would have to break off the engagement.

But that night he had a dream. And in the dream God's messenger-angel spoke to him:

'Don't break off your engagement to Mary,' the angel said. 'She has done nothing wrong. God has chosen her to be the mother of his Son – the promised King. You are to call the baby Jesus (the Saviour), because he is going to save his people from their sins.'

When Joseph woke up, it was as if a great weight had been lifted from his mind. It didn't matter what anyone said! He would marry Mary and take care of her and the baby.

Not long after this the Roman Emperor, Augustus, issued an order. Everyone in the Roman Empire must register at the town his family came from. Augustus wanted to make sure he had everyone on his list, and that they paid their taxes!

Joseph's family was descended from King David. So he had to go to Bethlehem, where King David was born. He had to take Mary on the long journey south through the hills – eighty miles of rough dirt roads. The donkey carried their food, warm cloaks for the chilly nights, and clothes for the baby who was due to be born any day.

Mary was very tired when they arrived at last. And there was nowhere for them to stay. The inn was already crowded with travellers. The inn-keeper felt sorry for Mary – but the only space he had left was the stable. It was dirty and smelly in there with the animals. But at least Mary could rest – and there was nowhere else.

That night Mary's baby son was born. She wrapped him up warmly in the clothes she had made, and put him in a manger to sleep.

On the hills around the town, shepherds kept watch, looking after their flocks. The night was dark and everything was quiet – just a little bleat now and then from one of the sheep.

Then suddenly there was a blaze of light – so bright, the men had to shield their eyes. And out of the brightness came the voice of God's messenger-angel.

'Don't be afraid. I've come with good news – for you and all the world. The Saviour has come – God's promised King – born today in Bethlehem. You will find the baby asleep in a manger.'

Then the shepherds saw a great crowd of angels, all singing praises to God.

'Glory to God in heaven,' they sang, 'and peace to all who love him on earth.'

'Good News!'

From *The Lion Storyteller Bible*

BOB HARTMAN

'Good news!' said the angel to a girl named Mary. 'God is sending Someone Special into the world. He will be a great king. His name will be Jesus. And guess what? God wants you to be his mother!'

'Good news!' said the angel to a carpenter named Joseph. 'God is sending Someone Special into the world. He will rescue everyone from the wrong things they have done. He will be God's own Son! But guess what? God wants you to take his mother Mary as your wife, and raise little Jesus as your own.'

'Bad news!' sighed Joseph to Mary. 'The rulers of our country want to count us, to see how many of us there are. And to make it easier for them, we have to go back to our home town. That means a trip all the way from Nazareth to Bethlehem! And with the baby due so soon...'

'Bad news!' sighed the innkeeper, shaking his head. 'There's not one room left in Bethlehem. But seeing as the young lady's expecting and all, why don't you spend the night in my stable?'

'Good news!' smiled Joseph, handing the baby to Mary. 'It's a boy, just as God promised. God's own Son, there in your arms – Jesus.'

'Good news!' called the angel to the shepherds on the hill. 'God has sent Someone Special into the world. The someone you have been waiting for. If you hurry into Bethlehem, you can see him for yourselves. He's just a baby now, wrapped up warmly and lying in a manger. But one day he will save you from all that is wrong. One day he will bring you peace!'

Then the angels filled the sky with a good news song. The shepherds went to Bethlehem and made a good news visit. And, on that very first Christmas Day, Mary just watched, and rocked her baby, and smiled a good news smile!

From Christmas to Easter

PAT ALEXANDER

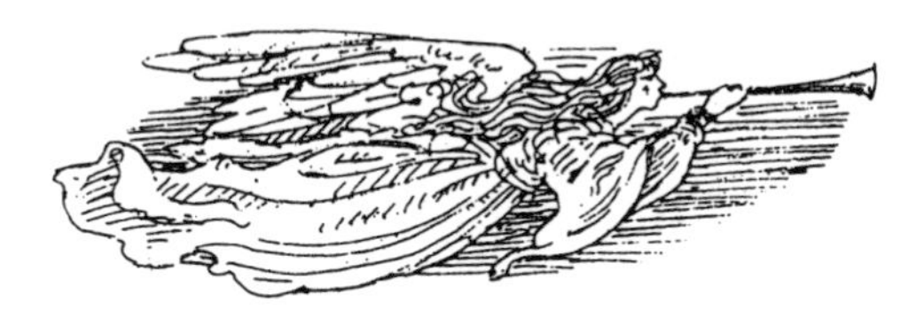

God's great rescue plan began with the birth of a baby. Not born to a King and Queen, or a President, or a Prime Minister. Not born in a palace or a castle or a mansion. No. A refugee baby, whose parents were poor and worked hard for their living. As Jesus grew older his mother Mary would teach him how to grind flour to make bread. Joseph the carpenter would teach him how to smooth wood with a plane. Most important of all, he would learn from them both about loving and pleasing God, his Father.

Jesus was a Jew, so his teachers taught him the Bible. The synagogue was his school on weekdays and his church on the Sabbath.* He was always asking questions. But in all the years he was growing up in the busy little town of Nazareth, no one but his parents dreamed he was the one God had sent to rescue and save them all.

Then one day, when he was quite grown-up, he knew the time had come: the time to leave home; the time to start his work for God.

'Good News! Good News!' Jesus said to all the people who came to hear him. 'God wants you to come out of the darkness and enjoy the light. God wants you to be happy. God wants you for his friends. He wants to set you free – free from sadness, free from badness. There's a special place for you in God's Kingdom. So get ready! Show him that you really mean it. Stop cheating and hurting one another – all the things you know are wrong.'

People came from far and near to listen to Jesus. He made God seem so close to them.

And he didn't just talk. He showed them how much God loved them by making sick people well. Yes, he made blind people see and lame people walk! One day he even made one boy's meal enough to feed 5000 hungry people. He did the most amazing things.

* The Jewish Sabbath starts at sunset on Friday and ends at sunset on Saturday.

And people loved him. Not just his twelve close friends, but many, many people all over the country.

Many, but not everyone. Although he was good and kind and never did anything wrong, he had enemies. Some of the religious leaders and teachers were jealous of him. They couldn't believe he was really sent to them by God.

For about three years the grown-up Jesus, with his twelve close friends, travelled the country telling everyone God's Good News, and making sick people well. For three years his enemies kept their eye on him, trying to catch him out, asking trick questions, setting traps for him.

Jesus knew that one day, soon, they would find some reason to arrest him. He knew that he would die.

'I am the good shepherd,' he said, 'willing to die for the sheep... No one takes my life away from me. I give it up of my own free will.'

He knew it had to happen. It was part of God's plan to deal with badness once and for all. And so, in the springtime of the year, as the time for the Passover Festival drew near, he set out for the city of Jerusalem. His friends were anxious for him. They did not want him to go. They knew it was dangerous. They knew that in the city of Jerusalem his enemies were lying in wait...

3

'Hurrah for the King!'

The Sunday before Easter is called Palm Sunday.
That was the day when Jesus rode into Jerusalem, with crowds of excited people waving branches of palm like banners and cheering him on his way.
This section begins with a short retelling of the Bible's story.
But I have included Malcolm Saville's longer one too, for those who would like to know a bit more about it.
Jesus rode on a donkey, not a war-horse, because he came as the King of peace. So we have the donkey's story here, and Ann Pilling's *The Donkey's Day Out*, to bring it up to the present day.

The King Rides In

From *The Lion Children's Bible*

PAT ALEXANDER

This story comes from Mark's Gospel, chapter 11.

Jesus was close to Jerusalem now. He wanted to be there for the Passover Festival. Jesus spoke to two of his friends.

'Go ahead to the next village,' he said. 'You'll find a donkey tied up there. It has never been ridden. Untie it and bring it to me. If anyone asks what you're doing, tell them I sent you.'

The two men brought the donkey to Jesus. Then they threw their coats across the donkey's back and helped Jesus to mount.

People were crowding into Jerusalem. As soon as they heard Jesus was coming, they came out to meet him. Some of them spread their coats on the road in front of him. Others cut branches of palm.

'Here comes God's King,' they shouted. 'Praise God!'

So Jesus rode into the city like a King – but one who comes in peace.

He went to the Temple, and when he saw the men selling pigeons for sacrifice, and money-changers giving out the special Temple coins, he was very angry. They were cheating people who had come to worship God.

'God's Temple is a place of prayer,' Jesus cried. 'But you have made it into a robber's den.' Then he overturned their tables and drove them out. The place was in an uproar.

Some of Jesus' enemies were the priests, and they were angrier than ever. Jesus must be arrested – but how?

Jesus' Last Week Begins

From *King of Kings*

MALCOLM SAVILLE

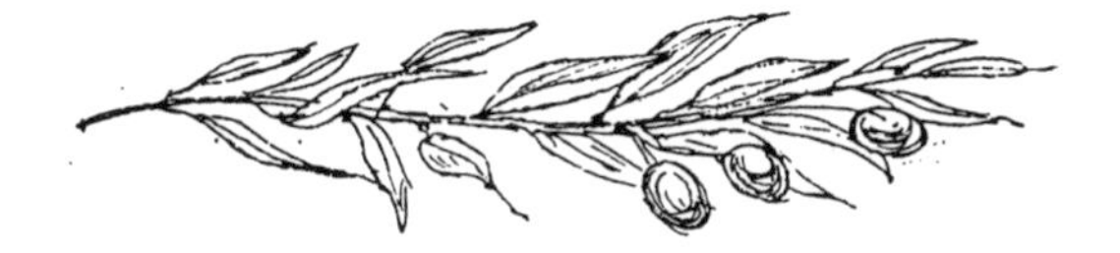

The road from Jericho to Jerusalem was a hard end to a long pilgrimage. It climbed steeply upwards through rocky ravines some 2,000 feet above the steaming Jordan Valley which is below sea level... Six days before the Feast of the Passover, Jesus and his twelve chosen friends arrived at Bethany on the lower slopes of the Mount of Olives, and, as usual, rested there.

They were all exhausted and thankful to be away from the crowds of pilgrims, and with their friends again. Yet they could not shake off their feelings of anxiety and apprehension. The disciples saw the sadness in Jesus' face with a sense of foreboding, although they could not believe he had come back to Jerusalem to die a criminal's death. Martha, busy with her usual welcome, noticed nothing unusual about this meeting, but Mary did. During the evening meal on the following day, which was the Sabbath, she did something very remarkable. From her room she brought an alabaster box of ointment known as spikenard. (It was sometimes customary in those days to greet an honoured guest by anointing his head with perfumed oil or ointment.) Mary poured the costly and precious ointment over Jesus' feet, and wiped them lovingly with her long hair. The disciples were upset and angry at this act of wanton extravagance. Loudest in his criticism was Judas Iscariot, who was in charge of their funds and looked after their simple needs. The ointment could have been sold for a large sum of money – enough to keep them all for nearly a month – or given to the poor. But Judas had less honourable intentions. Though no one knew it, he had taken money from the disciples' funds before now.

Jesus silenced their protests. 'What Mary has done is good,' he said. 'The poor will always be there, but I won't be with you always. Mary has anointed my body ready for burial. And I tell you that the story of what she has done today will be told wherever the good news is preached.'

Judas was unusually silent for the rest of the evening. Until now he had been hoping against hope that Jesus would declare himself as the Messiah and lead a revolt against Rome. Judas... had joined the twelve because he was a zealot in the rebel cause. But this remark of Jesus about his burial, coming after all his references to a kingdom which was not of this world, disillusioned him. His hopes dwindled and vanished. Bitterness filled his heart and darkened his thoughts.

In Jerusalem there was an atmosphere of intense excitement. The Feast of the Passover was the most important festival of the Jewish year. There was no room in the city itself for all the pilgrims. Over a million people were camping in the country around, many of them crowding into Jerusalem every day to the Temple to make their sacrifice. Jesus' name was generally known and there were many rumours about his miracles and his unusual teaching...

But to the Romans he was of little significance. He did not seem to be dangerous...

Pilate, Jerusalem's Roman governor, was always glad when Passover week was over. The Jews were an excitable race with a complex religion and liable to make trouble for him at the times of their peculiar festivals.

The real enemies of Jesus were the political and religious leaders of his own race who held power under Rome. These 'chief priests' worked through a council called the Sanhedrin in Jerusalem, but they did more than lay down *religious* law. They were political as well, and were in fact the rulers of the scattered Jewish nation. The Sanhedrin consisted of these priests and representatives of the Sadducees and Pharisees, together with the scribes who were experts on the law. These were the men who hated and feared Jesus, and were prepared to go to any lengths to get rid of him... Much of the teaching of Jesus to them seemed blasphemy.

And so, even before Jesus and his disciples arrived at Bethany on the Friday before the Passover, the chief priests heard that many of the pilgrims already pouring into Jerusalem were asking about Jesus and wondering whether he would come this year. This time they showed their hand, convinced that they dare not risk his presence and his teaching any longer. They issued instructions that if anyone saw Jesus or could find out where he was staying they were to be told, so that they could take him prisoner.

It couldn't have been long before the excited pilgrims heard that Jesus was in Bethany...

Next morning, when the people were crowding expectantly into the village in the hope of seeing Jesus... the twelve were hoping against hope that at last their Master would declare himself in some dramatic way. Surely this was the moment to enter Jerusalem in triumph – now, when the crowds were really with him?... Surely everyone would rise and acclaim him now?

Jesus knew what the disciples wanted. It was time for him to enter Jerusalem publicly, in solemn triumph. But it would not be what so many of his followers expected. He would not come as the leader of a rebel army, but as a figure of peace. He called two of his disciples and gave them clear instructions:

'Go ahead to the next village,' he said. 'You'll find an unbroken colt tethered there. Untie it and bring it here. If anyone asks you what you're doing, tell them I need the colt and they'll let you take it.'

The two men ran off excitedly and it was exactly as he had said. They found the colt tied outside a door at a place where two ways met. When some who were standing there asked what they were doing they repeated what Jesus had told them to say, and the men made no further objection. Then they went back to Jesus and the waiting crowds.

When the people saw the colt they remembered the words of the prophet Zechariah, spoken long years before: 'Tell the city of Jerusalem. Your King is coming. He is coming humbly riding a donkey, on a colt, the foal of a donkey.'

Now the twelve were really excited, for surely they would be able to share a little of his triumph? The news spread like a forest fire through the excited crowds. Jesus was going to ride in triumph into Jerusalem! He was going to proclaim himself the Messiah! He was indeed the Son of David, and this was the day for which they had been waiting so long.

There was no saddle for the colt, so the disciples put some cloaks on his back. Jesus mounted the donkey, and surrounded by his joyful and excited friends, led the cheering procession towards Jerusalem. The wayside was thick with flowers and the palm trees green with their heavy branches. Some of the crowd ran ahead and tore down the branches and carried them in triumph. Some spread them with their cloaks on the path as they would have done for a king.

As the procession moved forward they shouted in excitement and joy;

'Praise to David's Son! God bless him who comes in the name of the Lord! Praise be to God!'

As Jesus rode on, those nearest to him noticed that his face was sad. There was little sign that here was an all-conquering, popular hero coming to lead his people in rebellion against Rome.

Jesus had tried so hard to make them understand that there was nothing of earthly power about the kingdom he preached. They had already forgotten of his warnings about what was going to happen this week, and very soon now their dreams were to be shattered.

Soon they reached a bend in the road from which they were able to see the glorious city in the sunshine. No Jew could see Jerusalem unmoved. This time Jesus saw more crowds coming out to meet him, and although he was surrounded by those who thought they were his friends he had never felt so alone.

Some of his followers realized the significance of his deliberate choice of a donkey on which to ride, but many had obviously forgotten that this humble beast suggested peace rather than the sword. Jesus was the only one in this noisy, excited crowd who knew that the truth was utterly different from their own materialistic ideas. The kingdom of God which he preached was to be in people's hearts, because put in its simplest way, the world can only be changed by better people and only an ever-loving and compassionate God can make them better.

'Entering In'

JEAN BARKER

I love rough City streets
their thrust and shove
friction and attraction of bodies.

I bask in outdoor cooking smells
shouts of vendors selling
cloth spice aromatic oils.

Colourful fruits succulent
piled triangular on painted stalls
offer garish beauty.

Buskers beat and pipe music
alive with passion and rhythm
compelling blood and feet to dance –
but today there is something strange.

An agitating press of people
wave palm fronds yell and elbow
lost children cry are ignored

terrified sheep run forgotten.
I resist this mad carnival
but am swept up caught held fast

by a peace that leaves me wordless –
and a power that leaves me trembling
together in one extraordinary Being
riding between street women and fish stalls.

Simeon's Donkey

ELEANOR WATKINS

Fig and his mother, Olive, were grazing in the little field at the side of Simeon's house. It was getting warmer, and flies buzzed about the heads of the two donkeys. Olive, as usual, looked weary. Fig was in one of his frolicsome moods, nipping at Olive's tail and then dancing away out of reach.

Early that morning, Simeon had once again tried to catch Fig and harness him, ready to carry wool to the village. Simeon was a farmer and he was also a merchant, a middle-man who bought and sold and bartered and haggled. He needed good strong donkeys, and Fig was one of the sturdiest for miles around. Simeon had had high hopes of Fig from the moment he was born, but now, when Fig was almost full-grown, it was still Olive who did all the work.

The thing was, Fig didn't want to work at all. He liked to graze and roll in the sweet meadow grass at the foot of the mountain, to trot and gallop around the field, to toss his head and kick up his heels. He liked eating and drinking, lying in the shade on warm afternoons and tormenting Olive and the sheep and goats. He saw no reason why this carefree life should ever change.

'You are a disgrace!' Olive told him often. 'We donkeys are meant to work. I have always been hard-working, myself.'

No one could argue with that. But, looking at his mother, Fig felt himself no more inclined for a working life. Olive was old and tired, worn out with a lifetime of heavy loads. She was always thin, but when fodder was short Simeon cut down their rations, and then her bones stuck out under her grey hide. If she moved too slowly Simeon beat her, so that she almost always had sore places which the flies buzzed around and made worse. Fig didn't intend to end up like that, ever.

So that morning when Simeon, huffing and puffing, had made yet one more attempt to catch and bridle him, Fig had been ready. His quick neat hooves and tossing head kept him just out of

Simeon's reach, and when there seemed a danger that he might be cornered against the goat-shed walls, he had played his final trick, which was to turn his back on Simeon and let fly with his hind legs. One hard hoof had caught his master on the knee, causing him to curse and swear and hop around on one leg, clutching the bruised knee with both hands. Fig had galloped triumphantly to the far corner of the field and laughed triumphantly with a raucous braying sound.

So Olive carried the load of wool, while Fig rested and nibbled the sweet new grass, and swatted flies with his big ears.

When Olive came back she stood with hanging head, too tired for a while even to graze. At last she turned and looked sadly at Fig. 'Sometimes I am afraid for you. All the way to the village our master grumbled and muttered about what he would do to you, after that kick you gave him this morning.'

'He'll have to catch me first,' said Fig jauntily.

Olive shook her patient head. 'He would be rid of you, if you were not the strongest, handsomest young donkey around here. Others have offered him a good price. He may be tempted to take it. After all, he has had no use of you at all yet.'

'And won't, either!' said Fig with a switch of his tufted tail. 'I don't intend to carry great fat men or heavy loads! No one shall get on my back! If you had been as wise as me, mother, think how much easier your life would have been.'

'For shame, Fig! It is a donkey's lot in life to carry heavy loads. I've served my masters willingly, even unkind ones like Simeon. And my family is of a noble line. My great-grandmother was greatly privileged among donkeys.'

Fig sighed. Now Olive was going to tell the story, yet again, of how her great-grandmother had been present at the birth of a great king, and had later carried the little king on a flight to safety from wicked men. He'd heard it all before. The story was meant to inspire him, but he'd only found it boring. He took another playful nip at his mother's tail and pranced away out of reach.

Now it was afternoon, when the sun was high and all sensible men and donkeys should be resting in the shade. Instead, here was Simeon coming with the bridle again, puffing and blowing and cursing and limping, his face as black as thunder.

'That scoundrel has short-changed me for the wool! I've got to get back to the village at once, before he finishes his siesta and goes off somewhere else.' He paused and looked at poor, tired, patient Olive. Then he threw a black look at sprightly young Fig, and shook his fist. 'You young jackass! It's you who should be carrying me this time! I'd beat the hide off you if I could get near enough! You wait. My son Ben'll be home before long and he'll soon break that contrary spirit of yours!'

Fig had heard that threat quite often before. But Ben never appeared to break him in, and Fig felt he must have left home for good, and no wonder, with Simeon for a father! The threat didn't bother him at all. He kept just out of reach while Simeon, sweating and muttering, harnessed Olive again and climbed grumbling upon her back. When they set off towards the village, the sandalled feet of the fat man dangling almost to the ground, Fig followed.

It was a pleasant change, being out upon the road and seeing a bit of life on a warm spring day. He sometimes followed Olive and Simeon when they took a trip, if he was feeling bored at home. His quick hooves danced through the dust, following Olive's plodding footsteps, and the sun was hot upon his back.

By the time they reached the village, with its mixture of strange sights, sounds and smells, Fig was glad to move a little closer to his mother and their master. Other donkeys and men, and crafty cringing dogs made him a little nervous. He even allowed Simeon to slip a spare halter over his head and tether him with Olive at the door of the man they had come to deal with. It would be easy to prance away out of reach when he was released.

Simeon's business seemed to take a long time, and sounds of a great deal of arguing and disagreement came from across the courtyard. The donkeys stood quietly in the unshaded heat, twitching their ears against the flies, shifting their hooves in the dust. Suddenly the shapes of two men threw dark shadows across their half-closed eyes. Fig drew back in alarm, his hooves clattering on the cobbles. The men were untying his bridle and Olive's, working swiftly and surely.

Simeon came bursting from the house, his face red and angry. 'Hey! What are you up to? Thieves! Those donkeys are mine!'

The men kept hold of the bridles. One of them said, 'We're just borrowing them. Our Lord has need of them. Don't worry, we'll bring them safely back afterwards. You'll be well rewarded.'

Fig thought that Simeon would put up a fight. But he only stared hard at the men and then said, 'Well, all right. Only I don't want them lamed. I'll wait here in the village for them.'

It gave Fig an odd feeling, walking off with Olive away from Simeon, with two strange men at their bridles. Simeon might be an unkind master, but he was the only one Fig had known. He was glad Olive was there, and moved a little closer to her side.

They walked along the dusty road, through olive groves and along unshaded stretches where the sun beat down strongly, until they came to a place where more men waited. The two men with the bridles led Fig and Olive up to another man and said, 'Master, here are the donkeys.'

The man got up to meet them. He looked at them both and smiled. He was not a tall man and wore ordinary clothes, but there was something more than ordinary about him. He touched Olive's head and said gently, 'Good Olive! Sweet, patient, faithful Olive! I am looking for a willing donkey to carry me.'

Fig felt Olive tremble, and he knew that she would be willing to carry this man to the ends of the earth if he wished. He felt a touch of his usual scorn towards her. She was so foolish, and just because this man had spoken in a kindly way.

But the man was speaking again. 'No, Olive, my love, my sweet one. Not you. You are already tired with carrying heavy loads. You have aching limbs and sore places.'

His hands tenderly touched the sores on Olive's back and caressed her dusty ears. Then he turned to Fig.

'Good Fig. You are young and strong. You have a stout back and sturdy legs. Will you carry me today?'

Fig began to back away along the length of the halter. He was held quite firmly by one of the other men, but there was still room to turn and lash out with his hindlegs. He had never carried anyone upon his back and he didn't intend to start now.

The man reached out and touched Fig's head. Fig stopped backing and began to tremble too. The man's eyes were as clear as the purest of pure water. He stroked Fig's ears and rubbed his head. He said, 'This one will carry me.'

The other men brought cloaks and laid them upon Fig's back and the man sat upon them. The weight felt strange to Fig but he was proud to carry this man. He held his head high and stepped briskly along the road to the city, and the man's hands as they guided him were gentle and loving.

Fig had never seen so many people as those who came streaming from the city to meet them, nor heard such noise. People surrounded them, followed them, went before them, shouting and singing. Garments were flung into the road under Fig's hooves and palm branches were waved in his face, but his pace never once faltered. At any other time these things would have terrified him, but the presence of the man upon his back made everything safe and right. Behind him, Olive followed, her tired old eyes bright and her head high. Fig felt that he could go on carrying this man for ever.

But all too soon the ride was over. The man dismounted at the gate of a tall building and went inside. But before he left he touched them both again and said, 'Thank you, Olive. Thank you, Fig. You have served me well. Now go back and serve your own master.'

They would both have followed him, but hands held them back. Desolate, they were led away through the busy, noisy streets, back to their own village where Simeon waited for them.

They had half expected a beating, but Simeon only inspected their hooves to see if they were lame, and, finding them sound, grunted with relief. Fig noticed afresh Simeon's fat, flabby, none-too-gentle hands and longed for the caring, gentle hands of the other man. But that man had told him to serve his own master, and he knew he would obey that man to the end. So he stood quietly while Simeon rather warily climbed upon his back, and then he carried him home.

Both donkeys were surprised at an extra measure of barley for their suppers.

'He seems changed,' said Fig wonderingly.

'We are all changed,' said Olive.

It was true. When Fig looked at Olive he saw that she seemed somehow younger and livelier, in spite of the dreadfully tiring day. She stood straighter and her eyes were brighter. And all the sore places on her back where the man's hands had touched her were perfectly healed, and covered with soft grey hair.

He knew that, because of the man, he was changed too. He saw suddenly how careless and selfish he had been. He would work, so that Olive could rest. The work might not be easy or pleasant, or his masters always kind. He would have to suffer heavy weights upon his back and maybe beatings, but he would remember always the man who had commanded him, that man like no other.

'The Donkey'

G.K. CHESTERTON

When fishes flew and forests walked
And figs grew upon thorn,
Some moment when the moon was blood
Then surely I was born;

With monstrous head and sickening cry
And ears like errant wings,
The devil's walking parody
On all four-footed things.

The tattered outlaw of the earth,
Of ancient crooked will;
Starve, scourge, deride me: I am dumb,
I keep my secret still.

Fools! For I also had my hour;
One far fierce hour and sweet:
There was a shout about my ears,
And palms before my feet.

The Donkey's Day Out

ANN PILLING

Fred was the donkey at Hoggart's Farm. He shared his field with three cows called Polly, Molly and Joan, who all had black patches on their broad white backs. Fred had a cross on his. When he was a foal he'd asked his mother about it but she didn't know why. 'All donkeys have them,' she told him, peacefully munching thistles.

That was long ago, and now Fred was old. Sometimes, when Polly, Molly and Joan were having one of their special cow talks, he would stand and dream under the willow trees.

He would think about the awful morning when he had been taken from his mother and brought to Hoggart's in an old green horse-box. How frightened he had been that day, how lonely, and how he'd longed to leap across the broad blue river and go back to his old familiar field.

But then Mrs Hoggart had come to see him. She'd tied a big yellow bow round his neck, patted him and said kindly, 'There, Fred, you look very handsome indeed. You're going to be a special birthday present for my son John.'

John's birthday party was in the paddock, under the willow trees. There was cake and ice-cream for the children and a juicy red apple for Fred. When all the food had been eaten, everybody took turns at climbing on to his back and riding him up and down.

John was grown up now and they called him 'Mr John'. Everything was changing. Old Farmer Hoggart and his wife were moving to a cottage in the village and Mr John was getting rid of the farm animals to make room for horses. They would jump high fences and win gold and silver cups. Some special stable boys were coming to look after them.

One day Fred woke up from his after-dinner nap and saw Polly, Molly and Joan being driven out of the paddock. The space was needed for one of the new horses, and the cows had been sold to Farmer Hill up the lane.

It felt lonely without his friends, and Fred was frightened. If all the animals were going to new homes, *what would happen to him?*

Every time he saw Mr John, Fred ran and hid. Very soon that old green horse-box would stop by the gate. He would be pushed into it and driven away to another farm.

One morning a horse-box did arrive but it was shining white with silver wheels. Mr John and William, the chief stable boy, were leading something out of it.

It was a young horse, jet-black, and he looked very scared. Fred saw him plunge and kick and shy away as they tried to get him through the gate. As he reared up the sun gleamed on his glossy neck, and his terrified eyes flashed fire.

Then the two men walked across the grass. 'Now,' thought Fred, cowering away, 'now they'll grab me and drive me off in that awful box.' And he started to shake.

But he was wrong. William caught the black horse, soothed him and let him go while Mr John patted Fred's tubby sides. 'Calm him down, old chap,' he said. 'He's a great jumper, but he's very nervous.' And they went away.

Fred felt proud and happy. He wasn't going to be sold after all; he was staying to look after this young racehorse.

'What's your name?' he said, trotting up to him.

'Tarquin.'

'That's a good name.'

'It's the name of a king,' the horse said proudly. 'What's yours?'

'Er, Fred.' It sounded silly, after 'Tarquin'.

The horse dropped his head and started to graze. They didn't talk any more then, but in the night Fred heard a little snuffling noise. Tarquin the Proud was crying.

'What's the matter?' asked Fred, snuggling up to him.

'I was dreaming about my mother. We were in a horse-box once. It crashed and she was killed. I miss her so much.' And a tear rolled down his nose.

'Never mind,' Fred said, 'you've got me.' To cheer him up he told him all about Hoggart's, and how he used to be Mr John's special pet, and how *he* didn't like horse-boxes either.

When the sun came up over the river they were still talking. Tarquin and Fred were already firm friends.

In the long summer days, when the grass was thick and lush, the two lived happily together in the field by the river. But when the cold weather started Mr John caught Tarquin and William leaped on to his back.

'Winter quarters for you, my lad,' he said. 'Your stable's ready, all snug and warm. It's fit for a king in there. Come on.'

But Tarquin wouldn't go when he saw that Fred had to stay behind and spend the winter in a broken-down shed. He bucked and reared and lashed out with his hooves till William fell off. Then he ran down to his friend, under the trees, nuzzling at his neck for comfort.

Three times William tried to mount Tarquin and three times he was thrown off.

At last he shook his head. 'It's no good, Mr John,' he said. 'That donkey will have to come, too.'

So Fred found himself walking behind Tarquin up the lane and into the new stable yard. From their stalls beautiful horses stared out at him, chestnut and white, and dapple-grey. But none of them was as beautiful as his own black Tarquin.

In their stable the straw was so deep it came up to his old knobbly knees, and there were food bags stuffed with sweet-smelling hay. There was even a heater for frosty nights. How different it was from his shack by the river, where mice scampered round his feet and gales blew through the cracks in the walls.

'Aren't you the lucky one, Fred?' said William, rubbing down

Tarquin's glossy black coat. 'This horse is going to be a real winner. He'll be running in big races one day.'

Fred munched the wonderful hay and tried not to listen. Tarquin had already told him about the high hedges and fences he would have to jump, how the horses sometimes crashed into each other, how the riders limped home on crutches with their heads all bandaged. He didn't want his best friend to get hurt.

Next morning he heard the clatter of hooves outside. The stable boys were leading the horses round and round the yard. They had rugs on their backs and funny little hoods to keep their ears warm.

'Walkies, boys,' shouted William, and they were off, away to the downs to canter and gallop and jump. In the cold air the breath from their nostrils puffed out like steam engines.

At first, Tarquin only ran in little races. Fred always stood nearby, in the yard, while they got him into the horse-box. Tarquin wouldn't go in unless Fred was there.

He ran so fast and he jumped so high that he won every single race. No one was prouder than the old grey donkey.

'Soon you'll be so grand you won't want to be friends with me any more,' he said rather gloomily.

'Don't be silly,' Tarquin told him. 'You're my best friend.'

When the spring came, Tarquin ran in his first big race. Mr John hired a very expensive horse-box and William was up before dawn, polishing and rubbing and grooming. When he'd finished, Tarquin's coat looked like a great black mirror. Fred stared at him in awe. He really did look like a king today.

They led Fred out and put him in the horse-box first. '*Me?*' he thought. 'There must be some mistake.' Then he heard Mr John whisper to the driver, 'This is a difficult horse and the old donkey calms him down. We want to win the Junior Gold Cup today. I'm not taking any risks.'

Tarquin whinnied with pleasure when he saw Fred. The special horse-box had thick padded sides, in case of sudden bumps and swerves. 'Fit for a king,' said Mr John proudly. And it was.

They talked all the way to the races, but when they arrived everybody forgot about Fred.

'Good luck,' he said, as Tarquin was led off to be saddled and bridled. Then the horse-box was driven to the edge of a field and locked up.

All afternoon Fred strained his long ears to work out what was happening. It grew hot and a man came, gave him a bucket of water and let down the door of the box. But he still couldn't go to the races. He'd been tied up with a strong rope.

In the distance there were loud cheers, then it was quiet again. People wandered about, eating ice-creams and hot dogs. Once a child came up and patted Fred, but her mother pulled her away.

'It might bite,' she said crossly. 'Come on, we're here to see the horses, not a silly old donkey.'

When at last Tarquin came back to the field there was a garland of flowers round his neck, and Mr John was carrying a gold cup. As they got Tarquin into the box hundreds of people came, cheering and clapping. 'What a race!' they shouted. 'What a champion!'

Fred was squashed into a corner to make room for another racehorse called Grey Prince. He was coming to live at Hoggart's too.

Tarquin talked to the new horse all the way home. He never spoke to Fred, not even when the donkey whispered, 'Well done.'

It was all Grey Prince now, and the races, and his garland of flowers and his big gold cup. Fred kept trying to join in but the other two just ignored him.

'He's young,' the donkey said to himself, 'and he's had a great victory. That's why he wants to talk to his new friend.' But inside, something was making him want to cry.

Now that Tarquin was a champion William kept him very busy running and jumping out on the hills, and he shared a new field with Grey Prince. Fred, still in the old paddock, never saw him at all and he felt very lonely. Tarquin didn't love him any more.

One afternoon two strange boys came up from the village, crept to the gate and looked all around. When they were sure that nobody was looking, they jumped into Fred's field and grabbed him. They had games to play.

One leaped on to the donkey's back, dug his heels into Fred's plump sides and went galloping round the paddock. 'Gee up, you silly fool!' he yelled. 'We're at the races! Can't you go any faster? No wonder you can't jump – your stomach's nearly touching the ground. You're an ugly beast you are, ugly and *fat*. Come *on*, can't you?'

Then the other boy joined in, running behind and slashing at

Fred with a stick. 'You're pathetic!' he shouted, as the donkey, sweating and panting, with his old heart pounding away like a great engine, lumbered round and round.

When he was young he could easily have thrown the boy off his back and chased the other one away. But he was too old now, too frightened and too weak.

'Giddy up, big head!' and 'Giddy up, cloth ears!' they screamed gleefully as he trotted here and there, while the sharp heels dug into his sides and the thorny stick cut into his back.

When they were tired of running races they jumped over the gate and back into the lane. Now that he was safe again Fred let out a loud 'Hee Haw'.

'Ugly brute!' one of them yelled. The other picked up a stone and flung it at him. 'Let's go and see Tarquin and Grey Prince,' he said. 'They run proper races, those two.'

After they had gone Fred limped slowly away and hid under the trees. When he thought about what the two boys had done, he wept. It was the unhappiest day of his whole life.

But one morning, soon afterwards, William paid him a visit. 'Come on, old chap,' he said. 'You're needed down in the village.'

'Who needs *me*?' Fred thought sadly. He was ugly and old and fat. He had a great big head and a loud harsh voice. He was useless – just something to make fun of and throw stones at.

Anyway, he didn't really want to go to the village; he might see those boys. 'Perhaps the milk van's broken down again,' he thought, 'and they want me to pull that old cart.'

But they went straight past the milkman's house and stopped at the school. Lots of children were rushing about in bright robes. 'Hello, Fred,' shouted someone, and one of the teachers gave him a carrot.

Then they helped a little boy on to his back. He was dressed all in white and he had a long black beard made out of knitting wool. On his head was a crown made of shiny gold paper. 'My name's Tom,' he told Fred. 'I've got the best part in our play. I'm Jesus.'

It began with a story, and everybody crowded round. Fred nudged forward too. He liked stories. As he listened he knew it was the most important one he had ever heard.

The children were going to act the part called 'Palm Sunday'. It was about the wonderful day when Jesus rode into Jerusalem on a donkey. 'Hosanna! Praise to Jesus!' all the people had shouted;

then, 'Behold, thy King cometh unto thee, meek and riding upon an ass.' The beautiful old words made Fred's heart almost burst with joy. This was about *him*.

When the story was over, the play itself began. William took Fred's halter and they walked slowly down the village street. All the children ran ahead, waving green branches. 'Hosanna!' they shouted. 'Hosanna to the Son of David!'

People doing their shopping looked up and smiled. One lady ran out of the fruit-shops to give Fred an apple; another came out of the grocer's with some sugar lumps. So many people wanted to stroke him that William had to stop.

'What a lovely donkey,' they all said. 'Look, he's carrying Jesus.' And Fred gave a great 'Hee Haw' for sheer happiness.

He forgot that he had been lonely, laughed at and beaten, chased round his field till he could go no further. God had remembered him.

And God must love donkeys very much, he decided, to have given them such an important job to do.

Today it was Fred, and not Tarquin or Grey Prince, who was carrying the King of Kings.

4
The Saddest Day

'Good Friday' – the day Jesus was put to death on a cross – was the saddest day. So why do we call it 'good'? You will find the answer in *Good Friday's Bad*, one of the Haffertee Hamster stories for younger readers. *The Death of Aslan* is another story that helps to explain why Jesus died.

In *Winners*, Australian author, Nan Hunt, imagines what might have happened to Jesus' cloak, when the soldiers took it away. And the lovely American folk story, *A Tale of Three Trees*, takes us all the way from Christmas to Easter.

The little story at the end is a true one, as Michele Guinness discovers what Jesus' death means for her, today.

The Last Supper

From *The Lion Children's Bible*

PAT ALEXANDER

This story comes from the four New Testament Gospels.

Two days before the Passover, Judas Iscariot, one of Jesus' twelve special friends, went to see the chief priests. He was angry and disappointed. He had expected Jesus to lead a revolt against the Romans. Now Judas was ready to betray him.

'I will lead you to him when there are no crowds about,' he told the priests. And they paid him thirty silver coins.

'Where shall we meet for the Passover meal?' asked Jesus' friends, on the morning of the festival. It was time to get things ready.

'Go into the city,' Jesus said. 'You'll see a man carrying a jar of water. Follow him to his house. There is an upstairs room where we can have our meal together.'

That evening, before they sat down to eat, Jesus took a towel, poured some water into a basin, and began to wash their feet. This was a servant's job, and Peter was shocked.

Jesus explained. 'You must be willing to serve one another, just as I have served you,' he said.

Jesus knew he would not be with them much longer. He was going to die. The friends could see that something was wrong. Jesus looked so sad.

'One of you is going to betray me,' he said at last. They were stunned. No one said anything for a minute.

Then John, who was next to him, whispered to Jesus, 'Who is it?'

'The one to whom I give this piece of bread, dipped in the sauce,' Jesus answered.

He gave it to Judas.

'Go and do what you have to,' Jesus said to him. So Judas went out into the dark night.

Jesus talked a lot that evening, and his friends never forgot his words. He told them how much he loved them – so much, he was going to die for them.

'I won't leave you on your own,' he said. 'God will send his Spirit to be with you and help you always. I am going back to God, to get a place ready for you. Then I will come and take you to be with me. Don't worry. And don't be afraid.'

Jesus took a loaf of bread, thanked God for the food, and shared it round.

'This is my body,' he said. 'I am going to be broken, like this bread – to die. And I will be dying for you.'

Then he took a cup of wine, gave God thanks, and they all shared it.

'This is my blood, poured out for many people. My death will seal the new peace between God and his people.'

When the meal was over, they left the house and walked to an orchard of olive trees called Gethsemane.

On the way there, Jesus tried to warn his friends what would happen.

'In just a few hours,' he said, 'you will all run away and leave me.'

'I never will!' said Peter.

But Jesus said: 'Before the cock crows at dawn, you will say three times that you do not know me.'

'I would die first!' Peter said. And they all agreed.

When they came to Gethsemane, Jesus took Peter, James and John in with him. The others sat down to wait.

'Come with me, and keep watch,' he said to the three. He was very upset. They moved in amongst the trees and Jesus knelt to pray.

'Father, if it's possible,' he said, 'save me from this death. But only if that's what *you* want.' Three times he prayed, and three times, when he went back to Peter, James and John, he found that they had fallen asleep.

The third time he woke them, they could hear voices. People were coming. Torches flared. The Temple guards, and the chief priests, led by Judas, had come to arrest Jesus.

'The one I kiss is the man you want,' Judas said to the soldiers. Then he went up to Jesus and kissed him. The soldiers closed in.

Jesus did not try to escape or to resist them.

But Peter drew his sword. He cut off the right ear of Malchus, the High Priest's servant.

'Put your sword away,' Jesus said to Peter. And he touched the man's ear and healed it.

Then he turned to the chief priests.

'Why have you come against me with swords and clubs, as if I were a criminal?' he asked.

There was no reply. The soldiers seized him roughly by the arms and marched him off.

Every one of his friends ran off and left him.

The soldiers took Jesus to the High Priest's house. Peter followed at a safe distance. There was a fire in the centre of the courtyard, and the guards stood round it. Peter joined them.

A servant girl walked past and saw him.

'You were with Jesus of Nazareth,' she said.

Peter denied it. He moved away. But she said to the others: 'This is one of Jesus' followers.'

'No. You are wrong. I'm not,' said Peter.

A little while later someone heard Peter's north-country voice.

'You come from Galilee,' he said. 'You must know Jesus.'

'I swear I've never met him,' Peter answered, sweating with fright.

Just then a cock crowed, and Peter remembered what Jesus had said. He broke down and cried.

The Slave-Girl and the King

ARTHUR SCHOLEY

'I told you the upper room was booked!' Debbie's master was shouting at her. 'You'd better hurry, girl and get it swept – they'll be here any minute.' He followed her as she rushed up the stone stairs. 'That Galilean teacher and his men took it for Passover meal,' he went on. 'They said they didn't want a servant – they'll probably bring their own. But you'd better stay on. They may want more wine. And they'll certainly need a slave to wash their feet.'

Debbie swept as fast as she could. The Galilean teacher! So she was to see him after all. Her owners had kept her busy all week, and she'd had no time to see the man they were all talking about. He was a great new leader, some were saying. He could even be king when they threw the Romans out. That ride into the city on a donkey – that had been a sign to his followers, everyone knew that. And then he'd been creating such a stir every day in the Temple. He'd taken a whip to those twisting moneylenders – good for him!

'Thirteen places!' her mistress was now bawling at her from the doorway. 'What are you dreaming about? And you'll need the big bowl, and a lot more water, if you're to wash all those feet.'

What would he look like? Debbie wondered. King, Leader, Fighter? She'd be able to pick someone like that out anywhere.

'They're here, coming up!'

Debbie finished filling the big bowl and glanced at the men as they passed. That man there, was that him? This one, then? Perhaps he'd come in later, when they were all ready – yes, that would be it.

The last of the men came over to her.

'Is that the water for washing? Thank you, I'll take it, then.' So they had brought a servant after all. Still, Debbie thought, washing their feet wasn't the job for *him*. It was the slave's job. But the servant was still waiting, with a smile. 'And the towel – may I have it?'

'Oh, yes, of course.' He tied it round his waist, picked up the bowl and went in. Instantly there was a murmur. Debbie crept nearer to listen.

'Oh, no,' they were saying, 'you can't do that job!'

'Just what I was thinking,' muttered Debbie. 'Any moment now they'll be calling for me.'

But no call came. She peeped through the doorway. The servant had already started! And he was talking to the men as he washed their feet.

'You call me Master and Lord,' he was saying. 'Well, then, if I, your Lord and Master, have washed your feet, that's what you should do for one another.'

Debbie stared. Lord and Master? Was this – could it be – the Galilean teacher, the one they said would be the new king? No, no, she thought, you couldn't be a king and a slave at the same time, surely?

Sentenced to Die

From *The Lion Children's Bible*

PAT ALEXANDER

This story comes from the four New Testament Gospels.

Inside the High Priest's house, Jesus was being tried by the Jewish Council. It was still dark when the High Priest's servants called them all together. They intended to put Jesus to death, but they wanted it to look like a fair trial. Witnesses were brought in – but none of their stories agreed.

At last the High Priest questioned the prisoner himself.

'Why don't you answer the charges?' he said.

But Jesus would not say a word.

Then the High Priest asked him, on oath, if he was the King, the Son of God.

'I am,' Jesus answered. 'You will all see me at God's side, coming with the clouds of heaven.'

'You have heard what the prisoner said. We need no more witnesses,' said the High Priest. 'He claims to be equal with God, and that is blasphemy. Do you find him guilty?'

'Yes, guilty,' they shouted. They sentenced him to death. But they needed the Roman governor's consent to carry out the execution. So, early in the morning, they took Jesus to Pontius Pilate.

When Judas heard that Jesus had been sentenced to death, he was bitterly sorry for what he had done. He went to the chief priests and threw the silver coins on the table. Then he went away and hanged himself.

Jesus stood before the Roman governor, Pontius Pilate. The Jewish priests accused him of treason, because they knew that Pilate would not sentence a man to death for blasphemy.

'He claimed to be a King,' they said.

So Pilate questioned Jesus. But he could find no reason to put him to death. Jesus had done no wrong.

It was the custom at Passover to give one of the prisoners his freedom.

'I have not found this man guilty,' Pilate said. 'I shall set Jesus free.'

But the crowd, stirred up by the priests, would not let him.

'Kill Jesus!' they shouted. 'Crucify him! And free Barabbas.' (Barabbas was a murderer.)

They made such an uproar with their shouting that at last Pilate gave in. He knew it was wrong. But he was afraid the people would riot and get him into trouble with the Emperor.

'I am not responsible for the death of this man,' he said. 'It is your doing.'

Then he had Jesus flogged, and handed him over to his soldiers to be crucified. Crucifixion was the terrible slow death the Romans reserved for criminals.

The soldiers took Jesus away. They dressed him up as a king in a purple robe, with a cruel crown of thorns, and mocked him. They spat in his face. Then they took off the robe and led him through the city streets to Golgotha, the place of execution.

Jesus was weak from the flogging, but they made him carry the heavy wooden beam of the cross till he stumbled and fell. Then they ordered one of the crowd – a man called Simon, an African – to carry it for him.

At Golgotha, outside the city walls, they nailed Jesus' hands and feet to the cross.

There was a notice above Jesus' head:

'This is Jesus, the King of the Jews.'

The hot sun beat down and Jesus hung there, in great pain. Yet he did not hate his executioners.

'Forgive them, Father,' he prayed. 'They don't know what they are doing.'

'If you really are the Son of God,' jeered the people standing by, 'save yourself!'

Two thieves were crucified with Jesus, one on either side. The first thief sneered at him. But the second thief said: 'We deserve to die, but this man has done nothing wrong. Remember me, Jesus, when you come as King.'

Jesus answered, 'Today you will be with me in paradise – I promise.'

Jesus' mother and some of his friends stood near. Jesus spoke to John: 'Take my mother home,' he said, 'and look after her for me.'

At midday a shadow passed across the sun, and for three hours it was strangely dark.

'O God, why have you left me?' Jesus whispered.

Then he gave a great cry – 'It is finished!' – and died.

At that moment the curtain in the Temple split from top to bottom. And the earth shook beneath the soldiers' feet. They had been tossing up for Jesus' clothes. Now they were terrified.

'This man really was the Son of God!' they said.

To make sure that Jesus was dead, one of the soldiers thrust his sword into Jesus' side. Then they took his body down from the cross.

A man called Joseph, from Arimathaea – a follower of Jesus – went to Pilate and asked if he could take Jesus' body away for burial. Pilate agreed. Joseph and a Jewish teacher called Nicodemus (another – secret – follower) wrapped the body in long strips of cloth, with myrrh and other spices.

Mary Magdalene and the other women who had followed Jesus from Galilee went with Joseph and saw him put the body in a new grave, a large cave dug out of rock. A heavy stone was rolled across the entrance. It was Friday, and everyone had to be at home for the Sabbath, which began at sunset. So the women went away to prepare ointments and spices to put on the body when the Sabbath was over.

The Jewish authorities asked Pilate for a guard. They put a seal on the stone. And the guards settled down to keep watch.

The Death of Aslan

From *The Lion, the Witch and the Wardrobe*

C.S. LEWIS

The Lion, the Witch and the Wardrobe *tells the story of Lucy, Susan, Peter and Edmund in the land of Narnia. It is winter all the time there because the White Witch has usurped the power of the true ruler, Aslan the Lion. The Witch has Edmund in her clutches* *(see page 21)* *and he turns traitor. To save him and all Narnia, Aslan offers himself to the Witch in Edmund's place. Lucy and Susan follow Aslan as he makes his way to the Stone Table on the hill...*

A great crowd of people were standing all round the Stone Table and though the moon was shining many of them carried torches which burned with evil-looking red flames and black smoke. But such people! Ogres with monstrous teeth, and wolves, and bull-headed men... Cruels and Hags and Incubuses, Wraiths, Horrors, Efreets, Sprites, Orknies, Wooses, and Ettins... And right in the middle, standing by the Table, was the Witch herself.

A howl and a gibber of dismay went up from the creatures when they first saw the great Lion pacing towards them, and for a moment even the Witch seemed to be struck with fear. Then she recovered herself and gave a wild fierce laugh.

'The fool!' she cried. 'The fool has come. Bind him fast.'

Lucy and Susan held their breaths waiting for Aslan's roar and his spring upon his enemies. But it never came. Four Hags, grinning and leering, yet also (at first) hanging back and half afraid of what they had to do, had approached him.

'Bind him, I say!' repeated the White Witch. The Hags made a dart at him and shrieked with triumph when they found that he made no resistance at all. Then others – evil dwarfs and apes – rushed in to help them, and between them they rolled the huge Lion over on his back and tied all his four paws together, shouting and cheering as if they had done something brave, though, had the Lion chosen, one of those paws could have been the death of them all. But he made no noise, even when the enemies, straining and tugging, pulled the cords so tight that they cut into his flesh. Then they began to drag him towards the Stone Table.

'Stop!' said the Witch. 'Let him first be shaved.'

Another roar of mean laughter went up from her followers as an ogre with a pair of shears came forward and squatted down by Aslan's head. Snip-snip-snip went the shears and masses of curling gold began to fall to the ground...

'Muzzle him!' said the Witch. And even now, as they worked about his face putting on the muzzle, one bite from his jaws would have cost two or three of them their hands. But he never moved. And this seemed to enrage all that rabble... For a few minutes the two girls could not even see him – so thickly was he surrounded by the whole crowd of creatures kicking him, hitting him, spitting on him, jeering at him.

At last the rabble had had enough of this. They began to drag the bound and muzzled Lion to the Stone Table, some pulling and some pushing. He was so huge that even when they got him there it took all their efforts to hoist him on to the surface of it. Then there was more tying and tightening of cords.

'The cowards! The cowards!' sobbed Susan. 'Are they *still* afraid of him, even now?'

When once Aslan had been tied (and tied so that he was really a mass of cords) on the flat stone, a hush fell on the crowd. Four Hags, holding four torches, stood at the corners of the table. The Witch bared her arms... Then she began to whet her knife. It looked to the children, when the gleam of the torchlight fell on it, as if the knife were made of stone, not of steel, and it was of a strange and evil shape.

At last she drew near. She stood by Aslan's head. Her face was working and twitching with passion, but his looked up at the sky, still quiet, neither angry nor afraid, but a little sad. Then, just before she gave the blow, she stooped down and said in a quivering voice, 'And now, who has won?'...

The children did not see the actual moment of the killing. They couldn't bear to look and had covered their eyes.

Good Friday's Bad!

From *Haffertee's First Easter*

JANET AND JOHN PERKINS

Haffertee is a soft-toy hamster. He belongs to a little girl called Diamond Yo. In Haffertee's First Easter *he is busy learning all he can about the mysterious Mr Jesus King, as the Diamond family gets ready for Easter.*

On Good Friday morning Ma Diamond was very busy buttering hot cross buns as fast as she could go.

Pops Diamond had been up very early to fetch them from the baker just up the hill, and now the whole family was enjoying eating them.

'Why are they called hot cross buns?' asked Haffertee between munches.

'Because they are hot, to start with,' said Ma Diamond with a smile. 'And because they have this very special sign on them.' She bent down with a bun in her hand and showed Haffertee the cross marked on top.

'It's a sign that says GOD LOVES US,' she said softly.

'Oh,' said Haffertee. 'How can it say that?'

'Well,' said Pops Diamond as he put down his second bun, 'today is called Good Friday. It's the day when we remember that God loved us so much he sent his Son Jesus into our world to give up his life for us. Although he'd done nothing wrong he was tried and condemned to death. Soldiers nailed him to a wooden cross and left him there to die.'

'Left Mr Jesus King to die?' said Haffertee in surprise, not really believing his own ears. 'Didn't anyone try to help him?'

Pops Diamond looked very ashamed.

'No, I'm afraid not,' he said. 'Jesus' mother was there all the time, loving him. But she couldn't do much about it. Most of his friends had run away because they were scared.'

Haffertee stood there frowning, thinking about all those people who just let Jesus die. And he began to get very angry.

'Good Friday is Bad!' he muttered through tight lips. 'Good Friday is BAD.'

'Haffertee's right,' said Diamond Yo, nibbling the last crumb of her hot cross bun. 'Good Friday is bad. It was bad for Jesus but it was good for us.'

She gave Haffertee a comforting squeeze.

'It sounds funny, Haffertee, but Jesus had to die. At least, *someone* had to. It was either him or us... We really deserved it. But he died instead. So it was bad for Jesus – but it was good for us, because now we can be God's friends. So it really is Good Friday!'

Haffertee was quiet for a moment as he thought about that. Then he stood up.

'I'm going out into the garden,' he said briskly. 'I need some fresh air. These hot cross buns are making me feel sad.'

And he wandered off into the garden and up to the rhubarb patch... He stood there for a long time.

Suddenly he heard some very strange struggling noises. It was Samson the tortoise – and he was upside down. He was twisting and kicking and trying very hard to turn over. It was no use, though, he wasn't getting anywhere on his own. Haffertee moved over to him quickly and began to push hard on one side of the shell. He grunted and groaned. He moved his feet about to get a better push, and at long last, with a great shuddering thump, Samson turned right way up again.

He nodded his head at Haffertee, said 'Thank you' and then plodded off slowly into the long grass.

Haffertee just stood there, puffed out!

He was very surprised when he heard Yo speaking behind him. She had crept out to see what was going on.

'Well done, Haffertee,' she said. 'Well done! You saw Samson in trouble and you helped him. That's what Jesus wants his friends to do. He tells us in the Bible that when we help someone in trouble, he is just as happy as if we had done it for him.'

Haffertee stood there, breathing heavily, for quite some time.

'Come on,' he said at last. 'Let's go back to the kitchen.' They set off down the garden steps together. He was thinking hard all the way.

When they arrived in the kitchen he said, 'Does Jesus have lots of helpful friends, then?'

'Oh yes,' said Yo quickly. 'Lots and lots.'

Haffertee reached for another hot cross bun.

'And will they all be eating hot cross buns today?' he asked.

Yo laughed.

'No. Not all of them,' she said. 'But they will all be thinking of him. This is a special cross day, you know.'

Haffertee finished his mouthful.

'I do wish I'd been there,' he said, still thinking about Jesus all alone. 'I would have helped him somehow!'

'Good old Haffertee,' said Yo kindly, stroking his head gently. Deep down inside she knew that Jesus had had to die. No one could have helped him. That was the bad news. But then from the same deep down inside a chuckle came.

'But after Friday,' she told Haffertee firmly, 'there is always Sunday morning!'

Haffertee smiled. He didn't quite understand what Yo was talking about, but he wouldn't have long to wait now to find out.

Winners

NAN HUNT

'It would be a pity to tear it – look how it's made. Someone thought a lot of him.'

The four soldiers were dividing the spoils. The messy business of the three executions was all over bar the waiting. The felons hung there, in a state of shock, on their crosses.

Marcus reached out to feel the material. It had a warmth that surprised him. There were bloodstains from the scourged back of the prisoner.

'The blood will wash out,' said his friend Augustus, reading his thoughts. 'Will you bid for it?'

'Let's toss for it. That's fairest.'

It was Marcus who won. He claimed the cloak with a grin at the losers. 'Shall we play on?'

'It will pass the time,' Justin said. 'It's going to be a long day.' He grimaced, glancing at the crowd. 'Listen to them! They really hate the guts of that one in the middle. They know how to hate, these people. Makes it hard on the families. If I had my way I wouldn't let the mothers and wives come to executions. Better give the three a drink now. See to it, Aquila.'

The man on the middle cross refused the drugged wine with stoic dignity. Marcus looked again at the writing over his head. It said he was King of the Jews. Kings and commoners were the same when stripped of their robes and symbols of office, yet there was something different in the eyes, the way he dealt with the pain, the pity with which he looked at those gathered round the crosses. Local politics touched the Romans only as far as it threatened law and order. The peace had to be maintained in all occupied countries.

The day dragged on. The eclipse, when it came, sent ripples of panic through the crowd. The soldiers kept wary watch on possible trouble spots. You could never guarantee that a riot would not break out that would embarrass the occupation troops and give the Jews a score point. Easy enough for a fanatic to slip away in the darkness once the crowd was stirred up.

Marcus tied his winnings – he just couldn't stop winning – in a corner of the cloak before moving confidently amongst the crowd. He appeared relaxed but his eyes missed nothing that was going on. He'd be glad when the day was over. Light was coming back to the sky now. He heard the cry, 'It is finished!', and swung round to look at the King of the Jews.

'So are you, by the look of you,' he muttered. 'And so is your kingdom.'

A message came from Pontius Pilate that the felons were to be checked. Someone wanted to entomb a body before the Sabbath. It would have to be done before nightfall. One of the soldiers thrust a spear into the side of the King, though he could see he was already dead. The other two were given the usual treatment.

As the soldiers prepared to march off, Marcus whistled up a sturdy youth to carry his gear. The lad didn't curse as some of the Jews did, at the mandatory responsibility of doing his mile. He seemed still dazed by the events he had witnessed, but fell into step with the marching men. At the end of the mile Marcus held out his hand. The youth shook his head and marched on. 'Can't you count?' Marcus asked.

'Yes.'

'How far have we come then?'

The youth gave the exact number of paces. There was a hint of defiance in his voice. 'The one you crucified told us that the Law sets us free only if we obey the spirit of it,' he added. 'I will take it to the barracks for you.'

'You've a rare one there, Marcus,' his friends teased, as they took their packs back from their carriers. 'How do you do it?'

At the barracks gate, Marcus pulled out the cloak and offered it to the youth. 'You might get something for this,' he said awkwardly. He didn't want the cloak or any reminder of today's doings. The eyes of the dead King still haunted him. He had forgotten all about his winnings, tied in the corner of the cloak.

'Shalom,' the youth said, hurrying off. Home was far away and he needed to get there before dark. He tossed the cloak in a corner when he got in.

Sabbath was over and life resumed for the Jews. In the house where Simeon lived his mother had found the cloak.

'What's this, Simeon? Where did you get it? There is blood on it.'

'A soldier gave it to me. I carried his pack more than the mile, as the Teacher told us to.'

'What's this tied in the corner of it? Did you know it was there?'

'No. It was late when I got in. I just tossed it in a corner. Let's have a look.' Mother and son gazed at the Roman coins in silence. 'I'll have to take it back,' the lad said.

'Perhaps he meant you to have it?'

'Not likely! Here, tie it up again and I'll take cloak and all.'

'It's a lovely piece of work,' his mother said, fingering the fine wool.

'Better safe than sorry,' Simeon said. 'I'll go straight away.'

The sun was shining brightly as Simeon hurried back to the barracks. He asked to see Marcus, remembering the soldier's companions had called him that.

'What cohort? Marcus who?'

'I don't know.'

'I can't go round to all the Marcuses. What d'you want with him, anyway?'

'He gave... he was with the soldiers on execution duty the day before yesterday. Tall, with grey eyes.'

'Wait here.' The guard called to someone inside and after a while Marcus came out.

'Yes?' he said impatiently. 'What do you want?'

Simeon held out the cloak. 'You forgot...' he began.

'No, no, I gave it to you.'

Simeon held up the bulging corner. 'This too?'

Marcus gave a snort of laughter. 'I've just won a wager,' he said. 'I somehow thought you'd be back.' He unknotted the cloak and recovered his money. 'Keep the cloak,' he said. 'That's yours. Did the King tell you to be honest, as well as to go an extra mile?'

'No, Moses told us that when Yahweh gave the Commandments,' Simeon said quickly. 'Blessed be his name for ever.' Marcus nodded and turned away.

The air had a bite to it in spite of the spring sunshine and Simeon hurried along to keep warm. He was glad Marcus had told him to keep the cloak. Even as he thought it, he saw a young girl helping an old woman along at a shuffling pace. The girl's clothing was thin and she was shivering. 'Here,' Simeon said, thrusting out the cloak. 'Wrap this around you. You look half frozen.' He smiled and dashed away before she could thank him. His heart felt strangely light, in spite of the grief that had been with him ever since Sabbath eve. What would the friends of the Teacher do now? Would they keep faith? Would they be scattered?

Rumours were spreading through the city. The soldiers guarding the tomb where Jesus was laid had been drugged and while they slept the disciples had come and taken the body away, and some of them were claiming now that he had risen from death. Well, everyone knew that was impossible, so it stood to reason there'd been some funny business, the church leaders were saying.

Hannah was grateful for the cloak. She had been deceived by the sunshine into thinking the day was warmer than they'd found it, and given her own shawl to her grandmother. The cloak was snug and warm. The two women continued their slow pace until they reached home. Hannah took off the cloak and examined it. When she found the bloodstains she was frightened. Where had that young man found it? She washed it carefully in cold water first, and hung it to dry in the breeze.

Later in the day, Hannah's mother called her. 'Take this soup round to old Lemuel, and don't dawdle on the way or it will get cold.'

'Yes, Mother. But if I hurry too much I might spill it!'

'You have an answer for everything, don't you?' her mother said. 'Off you go.'

Hannah checked the cloak as she went past the line and was surprised to find it dry. It had the smell of freshly-washed wool and sunshine, she thought, draping it round herself before picking up the bowl of soup and walking quickly but carefully towards Lemuel's house. The old man was glad to see her. People were always glad to see Hannah; she had a laugh that sent gloom out the window. She was dismayed to see how frail Lemuel looked.

'Drink it while it's hot,' she said. 'Let me help you.' She raised him carefully so that he could drink without spilling the soup. The cloak fell off her shoulders and she picked it up and wrapped it round the old man. 'That will keep you snug,' she said. 'I'll come in tomorrow to see how you are.'

After she had gone, Lemuel lay back, pulling the cloak round so his cheek rested against it. He dreamed of the village where he had been born, and childhood companions, and the special scent of the hillside in spring, and someone calling him home.

The women who came to prepare him for burial folded the cloak and laid it to one side. Hannah's mother recognized it.

'The little lass must have left it with him yesterday when she brought the soup,' she said. 'It was given to her by a young lad who told her she looked half frozen. She'd given Granny her shawl when the wind turned nasty.'

'You'd best take it, then,' said Elizabeth. She picked it up and stood transfixed. Her fingers stroked the cloth and her eyes filled with tears. 'It belonged to the Teacher!' she said.

'How do you know? How can you be sure?'

'Touched it. Clung to it. Believed in its wearer's power to heal through it!' Elizabeth gasped. 'How could I forget the feel of it?'

'It could be,' Hannah's mother said slowly. 'There was blood on it when Hannah brought it home. She washed it.'

'What shall we do, then? His mother?'

'Poor woman. I think we should ask Hannah, though, as it was hers after all.'

There were urgent feet on the stairs. 'Elizabeth, Susannah, have you heard?'

'Heard what? What's happened?'

'It's Jesus! He's alive! He's spoken to Mary Magdalene and the disciples! They have seen him! He is *alive*!'

The women were stunned. Weeping, laughing, hugging one another for joy, asking questions, they forgot about Lemuel. 'He said he would and we didn't really believe him! What fools we were! We thought he would live for ever as we knew him, and then he was crucified and put in the tomb and we thought our hope had died with him.'

'If only Lemuel had lived to know of this,' Elizabeth said. 'He would have been so happy.'

'He is happy,' said Susannah definitely. 'He died with the Teacher's cloak around him.'

They asked Hannah what she wanted to do with the cloak. She brushed away the tears she had shed for Lemuel, and stroked the garment with loving hands. 'I don't think it is meant to stay anywhere for very long,' she said. 'It's to fill a need and then be passed on. Even though it belonged to the Master, as you say, it is not to be stored in a chest, but to be used. It warmed me, it comforted Lemuel, it will find the next person to go when it is the right time. We must not make an idol of it.'

So the cloak passed from one person to another, bringing warmth and comfort wherever it went, and eventually disappeared from Jerusalem.

The Tale of Three Trees

ANGELA ELWELL HUNT

Once upon a mountaintop, three little trees stood and dreamed of what they wanted to become when they grew up.

The first little tree looked up at the stars twinkling like diamonds above him. 'I want to hold treasure,' he said. 'I want to be covered with gold and filled with precious stones. I will be the most beautiful treasure chest in the world!'

The second little tree looked out at the small stream trickling by on its way to the ocean. 'I want to be a strong sailing ship,' he said. 'I want to travel mighty waters and carry powerful kings. I will be the strongest ship in the world!'

The third little tree looked down into the valley below where busy men and busy women worked in a busy town. 'I don't want to leave this mountaintop at all,' she said. 'I want to grow so tall that when people stop to look at me they will raise their eyes to heaven and think of God. I will be the tallest tree in the world!'

Years passed. The rains came, the sun shone, and the little trees grew tall.

One day three woodcutters climbed the mountain.

The first woodcutter looked at the first tree and said, 'This tree is beautiful. It is perfect for me.' With a swoop of his shining axe, the first tree fell.

'Now I shall be made into a beautiful chest,' thought the first tree. 'I shall hold wonderful treasure.'

The second woodcutter looked at the second tree and said, 'This tree is strong. It is perfect for me.' With a swoop of his shining axe, the second tree fell.

'Now I shall sail mighty waters,' thought the second tree. 'I shall be a strong ship fit for kings!'

The third tree felt her heart sink when the last woodcutter looked her way. She stood straight and tall and pointed bravely to heaven.

But the woodcutter never even looked up. 'Any kind of tree will do for me,' he muttered. With a swoop of his shining axe, the third tree fell.

The first tree rejoiced when the woodcutter brought him to a carpenter's shop, but the busy carpenter was not thinking about treasure chests. Instead his work-worn hands fashioned the tree into a feed box for animals.

The once-beautiful tree was not covered with gold or filled with treasure. He was coated with sawdust and filled with hay for hungry farm animals.

The second tree smiled when the woodcutter took him to a shipyard, but no mighty sailing ships were being made that day. Instead the once-strong tree was hammered and sawed into a simple fishing boat.

Too small and too weak to sail an ocean or even a river, he was taken to a little lake. Every day he brought in loads of dead, smelly fish.

The third tree was confused when the woodcutter cut her into strong beams and left her in a lumberyard.

'What happened?' the once-tall tree wondered. 'All I ever wanted to do was stay on the mountaintop and point to God.'

Many, many days and nights passed. The three trees nearly forgot their dreams.

But one night golden starlight poured over the first tree as a young woman placed her newborn baby in the feed box.

'I wish I could make a cradle for him,' her husband whispered.

The mother squeezed his hand and smiled as the starlight shone on the smooth and sturdy wood. 'This manger is beautiful,' she said.

And suddenly the first tree knew he was holding the greatest treasure in the world.

One evening a tired traveller and his friends crowded into the old fishing boat. The traveller fell asleep as the second tree quietly sailed out into the lake.

Soon a thundering and thrashing storm arose. The little tree shuddered. He knew he did not have the strength to carry so many passengers safely through the wind and rain.

The tired man awakened. He stood up, stretched out his hand, and said, 'Peace.' The storm stopped as quickly as it had begun.

And suddenly the second tree knew he was carrying the King of heaven and earth.

One Friday morning, the third tree was startled when her beams were yanked from the forgotten woodpile. She flinched as she was carried through an angry, jeering crowd. She shuddered when soldiers nailed a man's hands to her.

She felt ugly and harsh and cruel.

But on Sunday morning, when the sun rose and the earth trembled with joy beneath her, the third tree knew that God's love had changed everything.

It had made the first tree beautiful.

It had made the second tree strong.

And every time people thought of the third tree, they would think of God.

That was better than being the tallest tree in the world.

That's it!

From *Child of the Covenant*

MICHELE GUINNESS

John Bunyan's famous book, The Pilgrim's Progress, *tells how Christian, carrying on his back the great burden of his failures, comes to the cross, where the burden rolls away and is gone for ever. Michele Guinness describes how, just a few years ago, the very same thing happened to her...*

I felt that God was sitting in heaven, judging everything I did, and everything I did was such a miserable failure. Could he ever forgive me? Would I ever be any different?... Then a school trip to York was arranged to see the Mystery Plays. A weekend away with friends was a rare treat and as the coach set off from Newcastle my pulse raced with anticipation. By evening the rain had benevolently acknowledged our pleadings and petered out to a light drizzle. Waterproofed to the hilt as only the English know how, we trundled in a straggly crocodile into the floodlit castle grounds, then found our places amidst dozens of other school parties. Someone handed out the toffees and chewing contentedly we huddled closer together to keep out the chilly evening air. I had not realised that the Mystery Plays were medieval interpretations of biblical stories from creation to the end of time, but somehow seeing the Bible portrayed like that as a whole made me realise just how much the New Testament was a continuation and completion of the Old.

As darkness fell and the lights on the immense stage beneath us were turned up, the munching and wriggling slowly stopped and the performance took on a magical quality. The crowds around me ceased to exist. The hard wooden bench which moments earlier had seemed to bite into my backside no longer vied for my attention. I was entranced, aware only that as we moved inexorably on to the crucifixion we were reaching the climax of the evening. Christ was on trial, was booed, hissed and rejected. A vast cross was dragged across the stage and the Roman soldiers stripped him and nailed him down with blows which resounded right across the York Castle grounds. As the cross was hoisted into the air with Christ stretched out upon it, suddenly everything fell into place for me, and I understood what I had been reading for the last few weeks. I wanted to leap up and down and shout, 'That's it! I've got it! That's why Christ had to die, for me, for my sins, so that I can be forgiven and have eternal life,' but I held on tight to the bench instead.

I was dizzy with excitement. All the self-reproach, the sense of failure and emptiness which had weighed me down for years and made me feel unable to look God in the face was offloaded onto that cross and hung there with Christ. This was the real freedom he spoke about. Blow the cost, I would follow him whatever it meant.

5
The Greatest Love

'The greatest love a person can have for his friends,' Jesus said, 'is to give his life for them.' And that is what he did on the first Good Friday – not just for those who were his friends already, but so that anyone can become God's friend.

The first four stories in this section are all about people who showed love like that. They are true stories. The last story, too – *A Life for a Life* – is based on something that really happened. The others are fiction.

The Greatest Love

From *The Everyday Book*

MARY BATCHELOR

This is a true story. It happened on 30 March 1945, the last year of the Second World War, at Ravensbruck concentration camp.

It was a spring day, a day of hope. But there was no hope on the faces of the prisoners who filed across to line up outside what the guards called the 'bath-house'. Every day at roll call, they would shout out the names of those who were to go there. Those who went never returned.

Life at Ravensbruck concentration camp was terrible. With only a bowl of thin soup and a crust each day for food, the prisoners were expected to work in the stone quarries outside the barbed-wire enclosure, or to chop wood in the forest. Some were forced to dig the trenches that would become their graves. They were there because they were Jews, and Hitler meant to get rid of the whole Jewish nation.

On this particular day, one young girl did not wait quietly outside the bath-house. She knew that a horrible death lay within, and she began to scream with terror. The guards moved threateningly towards her, but someone else was first at her side. Mother Maria, born a wealthy Russian, but by choice a poor nun, was at Ravensbruck for defying German orders and helping Jews in distress. Now she put a comforting arm round the young girl's shoulder.

'Don't be frightened,' she whispered. 'I'll come with you.' So together they entered the deadly gas chamber. Some say that the girl went free and that Mother Maria took her place.

The Soldier Who Took The Blame

Adapted from *Miracle on the River Kwai*

ERNEST GORDON

Many of the soldiers captured by the Japanese in the Second World War and forced to build the Burma railway died from starvation and ill-treatment. But the soldier in this true story gave his life, as Jesus did, to save others...

The day's work had ended; the tools were being counted, as usual. As the soldiers were about to be dismissed, the Japanese guard shouted that a shovel was missing. He insisted that someone had stolen it.

Striding up and down before the men, he ranted and denounced them for their wickedness. He worked himself up into a fury. Screaming in broken English, he demanded that the guilty one step forward to take his punishment. No one moved; the guard's rage reached new heights of violence.

'All die! All die!' he shrieked.

To show that he meant what he said, he cocked his rifle, put it to his shoulder and looked down the sights, ready to fire at the first man at the end of them.

At that moment, one of the prisoners stepped forward, stood stiffly to attention, and said calmly, 'I did it.'

The guard unleashed all his whipped-up hate; he kicked the helpless prisoner and beat him with his fists. Still the man stood rigidly to attention, with the blood streaming down his face. His silence goaded the guard to an excess of rage. Seizing his rifle by the barrel, he lifted it high over his head and, with a final howl, brought it down on the prisoner's skull. The man sank limply to the ground and did not move. It was perfectly clear that he was dead, but the guard continued to beat him.

The other prisoners picked up their comrade's body, shouldered their tools and marched back to camp. When the tools were counted again at the guard-house no shovel was missing.

‘Ring a Ring o’ Roses’

ARTHUR SCHOLEY

The nursery rhyme from which the title of this story comes describes the symptoms of the Plague, which killed thousands of people in past centuries, and was raging in London in 1665. This is the true story of what happened at Eyam, a village a hundred and fifty miles away in Derbyshire, England, that same year...

The horse and cart rumbled up the village street, coming to a stop outside one of the cottages that stood in a row, just past the church.

The carter jumped down.

‘Mrs Cooper?’ he bellowed.

‘Coming, coming,’ answered a voice from inside, and Mrs Cooper hurried out, wiping her floury hands on her apron. ‘What have you got now? Something for me?’

‘For your lodger. See the label? “Mr Viccars, tailor, Eyam.” It’s a heavy box – I can tell you that!’

‘Full of cloth from London, that’s why. Mr Viccars will be that

pleased it's come. He's been on the look-out for it this month past.' Mrs Cooper called back to the cottage. 'Edward! Jonathan! Come and give a hand – and tell Mr Viccars his cloth has come.'

The tailor was delighted. 'Some good stuff here, Mrs Cooper. Well worth the wait. Here, feel this. What do you say to a new dress?'

'Too fine for the likes of me,' Mrs Cooper replied, stroking the cloth with her rough hands. 'Maybe her Ladyship...'

'That's what I'm hoping.'

'Needs a good shake. Get the creases out – and the fleas! – before she sees it. Let me spread it out in your work room. It will be fine by morning.'

But when morning came the tailor had a fever and couldn't stop shivering. By night-time he was crying out in pain, so no one could sleep. Next day he was worse. And in five days he was dead.

'The Plague?' someone whispered, noticing the rosy red marks. 'Surely not, so far from the city?'

But soon Mrs Cooper's boys – Edward and Jonathan – were sick. Within days they too were dead, and the list of deaths grew. The villagers were terrified.

'We can't stay here, or we'll catch it too. We have to get away!' And at first that's what some of them did.

William and Catherine Mompesson, the new vicar and his wife, sent their two children to stay with friends. But they didn't go with them.

'Our place is here. Everyone is so frightened. We have to help them.'

Day after day the church bell tolled for more deaths. Men, women and children too.

The villagers gathered in the church. They wanted to run away. But then they might carry the Plague to their friends and relations. What ought they to do?

The vicar knew. He had prayed, and prayed too with Mr Stanley, the village's former minister – and now he knew what God was asking them to do. But it was so hard.

'Be brave,' he said. 'God is with us and will help us. We must stay together, stay in the village. Keep the Plague here, not let it spread. If we do that, we may die – to be sure – but many others will be saved. Do you agree? Will you do it?'

There was a long, long silence. Every face was sad. Tears rolled down many cheeks. But in the end the people spoke with one voice:

'Yes, we agree. We will do it.'

Quietly they went home, wondering how many more must die before the Plague was spent.

Meantime they would do all they could to stop the infection spreading.

The vicar locked the church door. From now on all the services, every meeting, would be held out of doors.

Every Sunday he read out the names of those who had died that week. Then one Sunday his own wife was too ill to come. A few days later, he wrote the saddest letter of his life – to tell his children, still away with friends, that their mother had died.

Months passed. A year. Still the people stayed in the village, going nowhere, meeting no one from outside. Food was brought only as far as the stones that marked the village boundary. The villagers left the money for it there, then went away, coming back to collect the bread, meat and vegetables that the traders had left.

In the house where the Hancock family lived seven children died, and their father too. Only Mrs Hancock, who had nursed them all, and buried them herself one by one, remained alive.

How much longer?

Autumn came, and the power of the Plague began to weaken. Not as many deaths now.

December – and a whole month had gone by without one death.

Then the vicar spoke to the people who had lived through it all. So many lost, so few left.

'I believe... I do believe, the Plague has passed. Two hundred and sixty have died. Only ninety are left. But we have done what God asked of us – with his help. We have kept others safe from the terrible suffering we have known here. Many lives have been saved. It's time to unlock the church, to go in and give thanks.'

The Day the Robbers Came

JEAN WATSON

This story comes from China, long ago, but it too is a true story of 'the greatest love'.

In a village in the mountains of China lived a family called Chao – father, mother and their two sons, Han and Lee.

The village was small and the people were poor. But they all worked hard and managed to grow enough food for everyone to eat.

The Chao family, like everyone else in the village, lived on rice and vegetables. Every meal was the same. But on very special days there was meat, too.

The rice was grown in fields called 'paddies'. At planting time the paddies were under water. It was wet and muddy work. Cutting the rice at harvest was hard, too. But everyone helped.

One cold winter, life was specially hard. The rice had not grown well. So there was not enough food to eat. Soon the Chao family and everyone else in the village had no food left.

Suddenly a band of robbers came riding into the village! They were hungry, too.

They went from one house to the next, looking for food. They shouted and were so rough that the people were frightened.

The robbers searched every house in the village. When they found no food they were very angry.

They ordered everyone to come to the temple in the middle of the village. The Chao family came with the rest – all except Han, who was out in the fields, trying to find food. Then the robbers seized Lee and tied him up.

'Bring us food,' the robber chief shouted, 'or we shall kill this boy.'

The villagers were very sad, for they had no food to give the robbers. Lee's father and mother were the saddest of all.

Someone slipped away to tell Han the dreadful news.

As soon as he heard, Han ran to the temple. He looked at his mother. Tears were running down her cheeks. He looked at Lee and saw how frightened he was. He looked at the hard, fierce faces of the robbers, and he knew they would do what they said.

Han could not bear it. He knelt down in the dust before the robber chief.

'I beg you – let me die instead of my brother,' he cried.

The robber chief could hardly believe his ears. When he saw that Han really meant what he said, his hard face became almost gentle.

'Never before have I seen such love!' he said. 'I will not harm you, or anyone else in this village.'

Then he turned to his men. 'Untie the boy,' he ordered, pointing to Lee.

When this was done, the robbers left the village, and they never came back.

The Pelican

ANN PILLING

The castle stood on a great rock with a twisty flight of steps going up to it from the car-park, a hundred and ninety-nine steps the guide book said, and the children intended to count them all. They could see very little that day. The village, and the castle high above it, shimmered through sheets of rain, and the low clouds were caught on the towers like rags, making it look like the palace of the wicked queen in some old fairy tale.

Tom and Gillian stood in the rain and looked round. The only vehicle in the car-park, apart from theirs, was a van with one wheel missing. Even the ticket collector had gone home.

'I hate this,' Tom said 'Why did we have to come? Why couldn't we stay in the flat? At least we could have watched *Tiswas*.'

'We didn't come all the way to Northumberland just to watch television,' Dad said rather irritably. 'There's plenty to see here, when the rain eases off.'

'I wanted to go swimming,' Tom grumbled.

'I wish you'd shut up,' Gillian said. 'You've been in the water nearly every day. Anyway, nobody swims in weather like this. You are ridiculous.'

'I'm not.'

'You are.'

'Those steps look awfully slippery,' Mum said. 'The water's just pouring down them, look. I don't fancy climbing up there, not in this.'

'Let's go into the church then,' Dad suggested. 'It'll stop soon.'

At the word 'church' seven-year-old Tom went rigid. Rainy days on holiday meant being dragged round museums and stately homes, where all he could see was the bottom of somebody's anorak. And churches! He disliked them most of all. They were always chilly, and smelt nasty.

Everyone was feeling wet and cold, not just Tom. Gillian knew that her father was about to lose his temper. 'Come on,' she said grabbing Tom's hand and running across the car-park with him. 'At least it'll be dry inside.'

In the church someone was playing the organ. The two children wandered aimlessly up and down the pews while their parents read the notices on the pictures and old carvings, and looked at the memorials. Then Tom spotted something at the front, and ran up to a brass lectern that held an enormous Bible.

He said 'Isn't it funny?'

It looked as though whoever had made it had changed his mind halfway through about the design. The outstretched wings were those of an eagle but the head was grotesque, wrenched awkwardly sideways to show a feathered profile. This bird was all beak, and there was a great bag underneath, dropping down from a head that looked too puny to support it. It was a pelican.

Tom was laughing at it, then Gillian said 'Look, there's a bird over there too.'

In the middle of the west window there was a pelican in stained glass. The bird stood on a nest full of open beaks and it was strangely twisted over, with its beak buried deep in its breast. Bright drops of blood sprayed down onto the heads of the fledglings and something was written underneath, in ancient letters:

'And so hir pelican
Of hir lyfe blud
Yaf to hir chickes
And help them with its gud.'

'What on earth does that mean?'

'The pelican gives its blood to feed its young,' Dad said, looking at his guide book. 'It says it's an old Christian symbol, but that it's really nothing to do with pelicans; it says it should be a flamingo, or something. It's a quaint idea anyway.'

'Ugh,' Tom said. 'I think it's horrible.'

A young man came down from the organ and went out, leaving the door open, and the children followed him. It was fresh-smelling outside.

'It's not raining so heavily now Dad,' Gillian said. 'Can we climb up to the castle?'

'All right, but we'll have to go carefully, and I don't suppose we'll see much from the top. I think we can go round the side of the church, and join the steps a bit higher up.'

They all walked through the churchyard, slipping in the mud. The path ended quite suddenly at a stone wall with a gate in it, and they were looking down a wooded river valley through which the water slid greyly, parting the green dimness of the trees like hair.

'It must be a marvellous view when it's clear,' Mum was saying, but Gillian interrupted. 'Look, down there, on the bank. That pink thing. It's a statue.' Dad got out his binoculars and focussed.

'Well I'm blowed,' he said. 'Look through these Gill.'

Through the misty rings she could see the figure of a bird. There was no mistaking the long scrawny neck and the bulging beak. It was another pelican. Tom grabbed at the glasses.

'*Don't* do that, Tom, you'll break them.'

'Ouch! Don't pinch my arm!'

The cry echoed down the still valley, and the bird on the flat stone moved suddenly; it opened ragged wings then took off, flapping clumsily downstream.

'Look at that,' Mum said. 'I can't believe it.'

'What do you think it was?' Gillian whispered. 'It really did look just like – '

Then a voice behind them said 'I know what you're talking about. You must have seen the pelican.' It was the young man they had seen in the church.

'We did see something down there. I thought it might be a statue, then it flew off. Could it have been a heron?'

'No, it's a pelican.'

Mum said 'But where did it come from?' and Tom shouted out, 'You don't get pelicans in England, except in zoos.'

'That's right. We don't know. It just appeared on the river bank, a year or so ago, and settled down here. They think it must have been migrating and that it got blown off course somehow. It's quite happy here. It flies up and down the river and keeps an eye on things. He's quite a character Percy is.'

'*Percy?*'

'That's right. The castle up there once belonged to the great Percy family, so it seemed just the right name for him. Have you been up there yet?'

'We were on our way, but it's so wet.'

'I'd wait for a drier day if I were you, then you can see

everything. You can row down from here to the hermitage, it's a stone cell cut out of the rock, and there's a good walk by the river, along that path, The Butts it's called.'

'Can you swim there?' Tom asked.

'You can, so long as you know what you're doing. Are you a good swimmer then?'

'I've just done my hundred metres.'

In the quietness the pelican had returned to its stone. Gillian watched as it folded its wings in after landing, and started pecking at its breast, like the one in the church window.

She said 'How strange that Percy should come here, I mean, to *this* church, with the lectern and everything.'

'It is strange. Everyone's interested in Percy. The vicar can tell you more, he's quite fond of him. I don't suppose we'll ever know where he came from, or why.'

The day they returned nobody could see the pelican. Gillian wanted to wait around for him, on the bank, but Tom was impatient. It was a glorious day and Dad had promised him a swim in the open-air pool that afternoon, when they got back to the holiday flat. They were going to practise straddle jumps.

There was only one boat, and it was out for the day, so they walked along The Butts and ate their picnic at the hermitage, a curious deep cell cut out of a massive sandstone bank. There was nobody else there. Tom and Gillian ran in and out, shouting loudly to make echoes, and standing under the drips that ran off the dank walls.

'Stay just like that!' Dad shouted. 'In the doorway. It's a really good shot,' then 'Oh *no*!'

'What's the matter?'

'I've left my camera up at the church. I must have. I took a couple of pictures from that wall, of the view down the valley. We'll have to go straight back, I'm sorry. Come on.'

'It'll still be there,' Mum said. 'It won't take us long.'

They packed the picnic away hurriedly and got up, but Dad was worrying. It was a new, very expensive camera.

'Look, we'll walk on ahead, the children will be all right. We'll meet you in the car-park. Don't be too long though. Keep your eye on Tom, Gillian.'

'OK,' Gillian said flatly, not wanting to be left on her own with Tom. He could be a little devil sometimes.

And sure enough, the minute his parents were properly out of sight he got his wicked look, and began to scramble down the slithery path to the water's edge.

'I'm going to swim,' he announced. He started to walk along the bank, peeling his clothes off as he went, until he was in his swimming trunks, looking down into a wide, shallow pool. He dipped a toe in. 'It's not bad. The sun's been on it.'

'Tom. You can't. You should never swim in rivers, and Dad'll be furious. He's taking you to the pool anyway, when we get back.'

'Oh shut up. It's dead shallow, look, I'm touching the bottom.'

He was in already, splashing about and doing duck-dives. The pool was patched with cool shadow and an old willow leaned over it. Gillian felt envious; she could hardly swim, but she would have enjoyed this. Through the dappled water she could see bright pebbles patterning the bottom. It really wasn't very deep.

The main arm of the river was beyond the willow tree, on the other side of a kind of mud bank. The water had cut a channel through it and it was just wide enough to take Tom, if he did a glide, and kept still.

And suddenly Gillian went cold. He was swimming through the cut into the main river. It was only a grey flash of water through the branches but she could hear it, swollen by all the rain. 'Tom' she cried. 'Come back! It'll be far too deep there, and the river's high. Remember what that man said. Don't be silly!'

'Why don't you stop fussing?' Tom's voice came back confidently. 'It's even shallower here, and I'm only on the edge. There's nothing to it.'

But she was determined to get him out. She grabbed at overhead branches and hauled herself up the willow so she could see him. He was now several yards away from the bank, making for a line of big stones that reared up out of the water. He was doing a lot of splashing, and trying to speak.

'I told you, it's all right,' she heard. But it was not. She could see that the water had already got hold of him, had snatched at his feet. He was at a bend in the stream where the land dropped suddenly down, and the water boiled and frothed over the stones. *'Gill,'* he was calling 'Gill... I can't ...' then *'Get Dad!'* in a muffled shout.

She watched the river take him and turn him over. He was so small. She thought there was blood on his face. He didn't seem to be moving down much, just threshing his legs wildly, half on his back, trying to grab at a bit of fencing on the far bank, that dipped into the water. She thought of that boy at their school who'd nearly drowned in a swimming pool. She had seen the ambulance men take him away, his face green-white under the dark-red stretcher blanket. That was why she was frightened of the water.

She tried to speak to Tom but no words would come out. It was as if all time had halted and the world was suddenly frozen, the trees, the sunlit river, the pink legs waving, and she was helpless with the horror of it.

Then something brushed past her face and she heard a strange, high crying. Through the grey-green willow branches she could see Tom jerking away from the big stones, trying to fling himself at the shattered piece of fencing that half floated out from the river bank. A great bird had covered the water with its wings and seemed to be wrenching something with its beak. She could see nothing clearly, only a flurry of pinkish feathers all mixed up with leaves and Tom's head and back, his fingers clawing at the fence-posts on the bank, where the river was lapping at the rusty barbed-wire turning the water a dirty red. She could see the small, bright eyes of the bird as it moved between the river and the land, tugging and straining, not letting go, uttering its shrill urgent cry.

'I'm here, don't worry,' a voice said on the far side, and she saw someone in a bright blue anorak leaning out towards Tom. 'You his sister? Your dad's coming.'

She must have been screaming. Suddenly the scene exploded round her head and she could hear her own voice in a tight shout, endless echoing down a long, long canyon 'Tom! Tom! Help him someone! Dad, where are you?' And almost at once her father was there, and Mum seemed to be crying, and somebody on the far side was helping the blue man wrap Tom in what looked like an enormous coat.

They had to spend the night in the village, at a pub called The Bear. The doctor came back to see Tom very early, before surgery, and told him to stick to swimming-pools in future. Then they sat over a large breakfast in almost total silence. Mum and Dad had been arguing in their room about having left Tom with Gillian on the river bank, and she kept seeing his face under the water, and feeling sick. The only person not affected was Tom. He ate a hearty meal and started to talk loudly in the public dining-room, about what had happened, till Dad told him, icily, to keep quiet.

'It's a good thing those men were there,' Mum said for about the twentieth time. 'And that they got him to grab those posts. They knew what they were doing. He wasn't ever in any real danger.' Gillian opened her mouth and shut it again. She knew. What point was there, now, in telling them what had really happened?

'I want to get in touch with them, to thank them properly,' Dad said. 'They were local, but they just pushed off when the doctor came. I could ask the vicar. He's still got my camera anyway.'

Late in the morning they went back to the church to wait for him. 'Funny,' Dad said, after ten minutes. 'He said he'd be here by twelve.' Then they heard somebody walking up the path from the river. The vicar came through the gate in the wall, slowly, with something wrapped in a sack in his arms. He looked solemn.

'Sorry you've had to wait. Had rather a sad find this morning.'

Gillian saw two spindly legs sticking out from the sacking, two yellowish feet, clumsily webbed. There was blood on the covering.

'It's Percy isn't it?'

'The vicar opened his eyes wide. 'How on earth did you know that? It is, as a matter of fact. I was walking the dog this morning, early, and I spotted him in the water, just below the hermitage. He was all tangled up in some barbed wire. Must have been out fishing, and got snarled up in it. Strange that, he knew this river so well. Looks as if it dragged him under the water, poor old chap. I had to go back for some wire cutters, to separate him from the fence. Vicious stuff that wire is.'

There was a silence. Then the vicar grinned and punched at Tom. 'This young chap's all right I see. That's marvellous. Enjoy the rest of your holiday, now. Oh, I'll just get the camera.'

Gillian sat in the church under the pelican window. The angular, shiny glass bird feeding its young looked nothing like Percy. She stared sadly at the bright picture, seeing, instead, the large bird, pinky grey, staring solemnly out across the water like a stately sentinel, with the gentle northern hills behind.

They would never know where the bird had come from, the young man had told her, or why, so suddenly, it had decided to live by the river. But she knew now, and she gave thanks.

The Substitute

From *A Tale of Two Cities*

CHARLES DICKENS

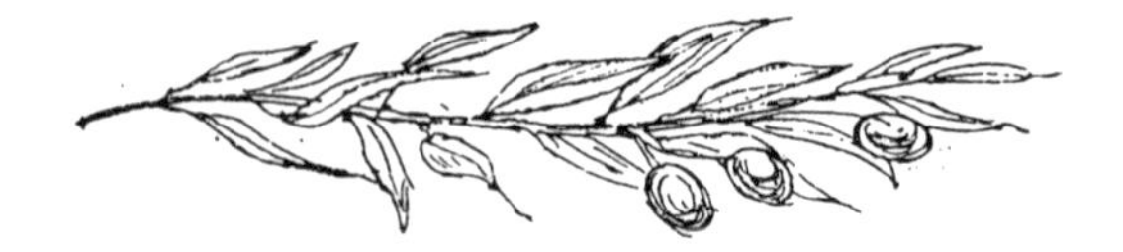

The story is set at the time of the French Revolution. Charles Darnay (really the French aristocrat Evremonde) is in prison, sentenced to the guillotine. Sydney Carton, who looks extraordinarily like Darnay, carefully plans his escape. For the sake of Darnay's wife, Lucie, Sydney Carton intends to take his place.

The hours went on as Darnay walked to and fro, and the clocks struck the numbers he would never hear again. Nine gone for ever, ten gone for ever, eleven gone for ever... Twelve gone for ever.

He had been apprised that the final hour was three, and he knew he would be summoned some time earlier...

Walking regularly to and fro with his arms folded on his breast... he heard one struck away from him, without surprise. The hour had measured like most other hours... He thought, 'There is but another now,' and turned to walk again.

Footsteps in the stone passage, outside the door. He stopped.

The key was put in the lock, and turned. Before the door was opened, or as it opened, a man said in a low voice, in English, 'He has never seen me here; I have kept out of his way. Go you in alone; I wait near. Lose no time!'

The door was quickly opened and closed, and there stood before him, face to face, quiet, intent upon him, with the light of a smile on his features and a cautionary finger on his lip, Sydney Carton.

There was something so bright and remarkable in his look, that, for the first moment, the prisoner misdoubted him to be an apparition of his own imagining. But he spoke, and it was his voice; he took the prisoner's hand, and it was his real grasp.

'Of all the people upon earth, you least expected to see me?' he said.

'I could not believe it to be you. I can scarcely believe it now.

You are not' – the apprehension came suddenly into his mind – 'a prisoner?'

'No. I am accidentally possessed of a power over one of the keepers here, and in virtue of it I stand before you. I come from her – your wife, dear Darnay.'

The prisoner wrung his hand.

'I bring you a request from her.'

'What is it?'

'A most earnest, pressing, and emphatic entreaty... You have no time to ask me why I bring it, or what it means; I have no time to tell you. You must comply with it – take off those boots you wear, and draw on these of mine.'

There was a chair against the wall of the cell, behind the prisoner. Carton, pressing forward, had already, with the speed of lightning, got him down into it, and stood over him barefoot.

'Draw on these boots of mine. Put your hands to them; put your will to them. Quick!'

'Carton, there is no escaping from this place; it never can be done. You will only die with me. It is madness.'

'It would be madness if I asked you to escape; but do I? When I ask you to pass out at that door, tell me it is madness and remain here. Change that cravat for this of mine, that coat for this of mine. While you do it, let me take this ribbon from your hair, and shake out your hair like this of mine!'

With wonderful quickness, and with a strength, both of will and action, that appeared quite supernatural, he forced all these changes upon him. The prisoner was like a young child in his hands.

'Carton! Dear Carton! It is madness. It cannot be accomplished, it never can be done, it has been attempted, and has always failed. I implore you not to add your death to the bitterness of mine.'

'Do I ask you, my dear Darnay, to pass the door? When I ask you that, refuse. There are pen and ink and paper on this table. Is your hand steady enough to write?'

'It was, when you came in.'

'Steady it again, and write what I shall dictate. Quick, friend, quick!'

Pressing his hand to his bewildered head, Darnay sat down at the table. Carton, with his right hand in his breast, stood close beside him.

'Write exactly as I speak.'

And Carton begins to dictate, distracting Darnay from the fumes of the drug which will leave him unconscious.

Within a minute or so, Darnay was stretched insensible on the ground.

Quickly, but with hands as true to the purpose as his heart was, Carton dressed himself in the clothes the prisoner had laid aside, combed back his hair, and tied it with the ribbon the prisoner had worn.

Then he softly called, 'Enter there! Come in!' and the spy presented himself.

'You see?' said Carton, looking up, as he kneeled on one knee beside the insensible figure, putting the paper in the breast; 'is your hazard very great?'

'Mr. Carton,' the spy answered, with a timid snap of his fingers, 'my hazard is not *that*, in the thick of business here, if you are true to the whole of your bargain.'

'Don't fear me. I will be true to the death.'

'You must be, Mr. Carton, if the tally of fifty-two is to be right. Being made right by you in that dress, I shall have no fear.'

'Have no fear! I shall soon be out of the way of harming you, and the rest will soon be far from here, please God! Now, get assistance and take me to the coach.'

'You?' said the spy nervously.

'Him, man, with whom I have exchanged. You go out at the gate by which you brought me in?'

'Of course.'

'I was weak and faint when you brought me in, and I am fainter now you take me out. The parting interview has overpowered me. Such a thing has happened here often, and too often. Your life is in your own hands. Quick! Call assistance!'

'You swear not to betray me?' said the trembling spy, as he paused for a last moment.

'Man, man!' returned Carton, stamping his foot; 'have I sworn by no solemn vow already, to go through with this, that you waste the precious moments now? Take him yourself to the courtyard you know of, place him yourself in the carriage, show him yourself to Mr. Lorry, tell him yourself to give him no restorative but air, and to remember my words of last night and his promise of last night, and drive away!'

The spy withdrew, and Carton seated himself at the table, resting his forehead on his hands. The spy returned immediately, with two men.

'How, then?' said one of them, contemplating the fallen figure. 'So afflicted to find that his friend has drawn a prize in the lottery of Saint Guillotine?'...

They raised the unconscious figure, placed it on a litter they had brought to the door, and bent to carry it away.

'The time is short, Evremonde,' said the spy, in a warning voice.

'I know it well,' answered Carton. 'Be careful of my friend, I entreat you, and leave me...'

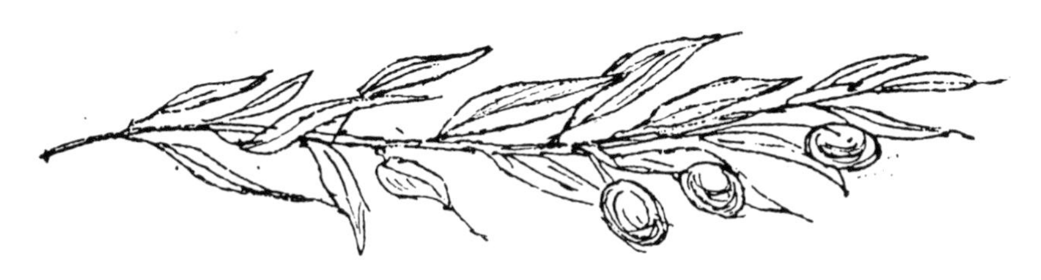

The door closed, and Carton was left alone. Straining his powers of listening to the utmost, he listened for any sound that might denote suspicion or alarm. There was none. Keys turned, doors clashed, footsteps passed along distant passages: no cry was raised, or hurry made, that seemed unusual. Breathing more freely in a little while, he sat down at the table, and listened again until the clocks struck two.

Sounds that he was not afraid of, for he divined their meaning, then began to be audible. Several doors were opened in succession, and finally his own. A jailer, with a list in his hand, looked in, merely saying, 'Follow me, Evremonde!' and he followed into a large dark room, at a distance. It was a dark winter day, and what with the shadows within, and what with the shadows without, he could but dimly discern the others who were brought there to have their arms bound. Some were standing; some seated. Some were lamenting, and in restless motion; but these were few. The great majority were silent and still, looking fixedly at the ground.

As he stood by the wall in a dim corner, while some of the fifty-two were brought in after him, one man stopped in passing, to embrace him, as having a knowledge of him. It thrilled him with a great dread of discovery; but the man went on. A very few moments after that, a young woman, with a slight girlish form, a sweet spare face in which there was no vestige of colour, and large, widely-opened, patient eyes, rose from the seat where he had observed her sitting, and came to speak to him.

'Citizen Evremonde,' she said, touching him with her cold hand. 'I am a poor little seamstress, who was with you in La Force.'

He murmured for answer: 'True. I forget what you were accused of?'

'Plots. Though the just Heaven knows I am innocent of any. Is it likely? Who would think of plotting with a poor little weak creature like me?'

The forlorn smile with which she said it, so touched him, that tears started from his eyes.

'I am not afraid to die, Citizen Evremonde, but I have done nothing. I am not unwilling to die, if the Republic which is to do so much good to us poor, will profit by my death; but I do not know how that can be, Citizen Evremonde. Such a poor weak little creature!'

As the last thing on earth that his heart was to warm and soften to, it warmed and softened to this pitiable girl.

'I heard you were released, Citizen Evremonde. I hoped it was true?'

'It was. But I was again taken and condemned.'

'If I may ride with you, Citizen Evremonde, will you let me hold your hand? I am not afraid, but I am little and weak, and it will give me more courage.'

As the patient eyes were lifted to his face, he saw a sudden doubt in them, and then astonishment. He pressed the work-worn, hunger-worn young fingers, and touched his lips.

'Are you dying for him?' she whispered.

'And his wife and child. Hush! Yes.'

'Oh, you will let me hold your brave hand, stranger?'

'Hush! Yes, my poor sister; to the last.'

The Friends

From *I am David*

ANNE HOLM

David has escaped from a concentration camp. He is on his way to Denmark to find his mother. But winter comes. A snowstorm drives him to the door of a farmer. And David is a prisoner once again...

David knew that he could never have lasted through the winter tramping the roads. He would have died of hunger and cold. At least he had shelter here, and food every day.

The stable was cold, and sometimes the snow was blown into drifts until it lay as high as the roof outside. But as it hardened, the stable grew warmer inside, and the animals added a little to the warmth.

He was not given much food, only dry bread or cold scraps, yet he had more to eat than in the camp, and it tasted no worse – sometimes, in fact, a little better.

They thought they were making him suffer by leaving him to sleep alone in the dark stable, but night was his pleasantest time!

David was not afraid of the dark. There were only common everyday objects about him, and the animals asleep. It seemed quite natural: the darkness altered nothing. What he was afraid of was people.

At night-time the stable was his. In the camp he had never been alone, and David liked to be left by himself to think in peace.

Then the dog came.

David had always thought of dogs as enemies – *their* tools. It was one of their pastimes to make the dogs bite the prisoners. Since his escape into Italy he had of course noticed that good people kept dogs too, but he had always given them a wide berth, just in case.

But shut up in the stable, he could not avoid the dog. It came one night when it was snowing hard and a gale was howling outside. David lay quite still and much against his will let it sniff all round him. The farmer and his family spoke a peculiar kind of German: perhaps that was the reason David spoke to it in Italian.

'I'm afraid of you,' he said softly in as steady a voice as he could muster. 'You're sure to notice I come from the camp, and then you'll bite me. And there's nothing I can do about it.' David could see the dog as it went on sniffing round him like a big black shadow against the darkness. Then it lay down by his side, pushing and turning until they were lying back to back. It yawned very loudly, then it gave a sigh and fell asleep.

It did not bite him, and David was not nearly so cold in the night, for the dog was big and kept him warm. It was called King.

It often growled at the farmer's children, and David knew it was not very fond of the farmer, either, though he rarely struck it, no doubt because it was a good sheep-dog, and in the summer when the animals were out to graze he could not do without it.

But whenever the dog saw David, it would wag its tail, and it went to sleep with him every night.

David gradually began to grow fond of it. One evening as he lay awake wondering if the winter would ever come to an end, he held his hand out to the dog when it came to lie down beside him. He did it without thinking. Perhaps he had missed it and wanted it to come and share its warmth with him. He found himself touching its head, feeling the roundness of its skull under his hand and liking the firm warm feel of it. The dog did not move, and David let his hand glide slowly over the dog's thick coat, just once.

Then he took his hand away and lay still again.

The dog lifted its head and turned towards him, and David felt its warm wet tongue carefully licking his hand.

And so David and the dog became friends...

At last spring comes – and David tunnels his way to freedom. But King, the dog, refuses to be left behind...

During the days that followed David got several lifts, and King learned to lie perfectly still across David's feet so that no one could accuse him of being restless. People were always nervous of him at first, for he often looked as if he would bite and he *was* very big. But when they saw how meekly he did everything David told him to, they would laugh and call him a sheep in wolf's clothing, for David always spoke very quietly and politely to him in a way they obviously did not think it possible to talk to a dog. But David did not care. King had chosen to go with him, and he was not going to show ingratitude by ordering him about. David hated orders himself, and loud commanding voices, and as long as he was with him, King should remain a free dog.

He was a clever dog, too. David had heard people say a dog was 'as clever as a human being', but that, he thought, was nonsense. A dog was a dog, and a man was a man, and you could not be as clever as something quite different. But a dog could certainly be clever in a doggy sort of way, and King was clever. And good.

Everything had been fine since he gave the farmer the slip and the dog joined him. There had been times, of course, when he was hungry and felt the cold; but nothing had happened to frighten him, and he had not seen anyone who looked like *them*, and he knew where he was going.

It was comforting to have the dog with him. He could not carry on a conversation with it, naturally, but it was good to know it was there, keeping him warm at night and always ready to protect him. David knew he could not rely too much on the dog's protection for though it could bite, it could not get the better of a man – not one of *them*, at any rate: they always went armed. But it was a comfort just to know it wanted to.

David was to learn his mistake.

Perhaps it happened because he was in too much of a hurry. He was able to plan his route from the maps he found on railway stations, and he had become quite good at working out how long a particular stretch of the journey would take if he got a lift or if he had to walk. He knew that it would not take him many days now to reach Denmark. Perhaps it happened, too, because for hours at a time he could almost forget his fears now...

He must have been walking for half an hour before he was suddenly aware of his fear and knew he should have sensed danger earlier. It was dusk and he had been too preoccupied with finding a good place to sleep.

Something was wrong. That building farther down the hillside... and the man standing outside it.

He called to King softly, in a whisper.

He had returned to *them*!

He lay as still as death behind a bush. It was fortunate King always did as he was told and was now lying perfectly still by his side. How had it happened? There was no doubt about it: he was back among *them*. David knew the signs only too well. He was only too familiar with the way *they* looked.

The dog looked at him questioningly and began quietly whimpering. David placed his hand over its muzzle and it stopped, but it continued to look at him. The bush was too thin, its new green leaves too small. David quite forgot how beautiful he had thought spring was, only that morning, with its small new bright-green leaves. His one thought now was that you could look through the bush and see him lying on the ground – and he was David, a boy who had fled from *them*.

In their barracks they would have a list of everybody who was under suspicion and should be arrested on sight. *Their* guards always had a list like that. On that list would be found: 'David. A thin boy with brown hair, escaped from concentration camp.' And under the heading 'Recognition Marks' would be: 'It is obvious from the appearance of his eyes that he is not an ordinary boy but only a prisoner.'

If the men had not been talking so loudly, they would have heard him already. They were much too close to him, and he would never be able to get away. Even if he waited until it was dark, they would hear him as soon as he moved.

His flight would end where it began – at the point of a rifle.

For he would not stop when they shouted to him. If he stopped they would not shoot, but they would interrogate him instead and send him back to the camp. And there, strong and healthy as he was, he would be a terribly long time dying.

No, when they called to him, he would run, and then the shot would be fired which had been waiting for him ever since that night when he had walked calmly towards the tree on the way to the mine outside the camp. But this time he would not be able to walk calmly away from them. He now knew how wonderful life could be, and his desire to live would spur him on. He would run – he knew it. And it would be a victory for *them*.

David remembered all the pain and bitterness he had ever known – and how much he could remember in such a short time! He recalled, too, all the good things he had learned about since he had gained his freedom – beauty and laughter, music and kind people... a dog to walk by his side, and a place to aim for...

This would be the end. He pressed his face into the dog's long coat so that no one should hear him, and wept. He wept quite quietly, but the dog grew uneasy and wanted to whimper again.

David stopped crying. 'God,' he whispered, 'God of the green pastures and still waters... You can't do anything about this. I don't mean to be rude, because I know you're very strong and you could make those men down there want to walk away for a bit. But they won't. They don't know, you see, and they're not afraid of you. But they are afraid of the commandant because he'll have them shot if they leave their posts. So you can see there's nothing you can do now. But please don't think I'm blaming you. It was my own fault for not seeing the danger in time. I shall run... Perhaps you'll see they aim straight so it doesn't hurt before I die. I'm so frightened of things that hurt. No, I forgot. I've only one promise of help left, and it's more important you should help the dog get away and find some good people to live with. Perhaps *they'll* shoot straight anyway, but if they don't it can't be helped: you must save the dog because it once tried to protect me. Thank you for having been my God: I'm glad I chose you. And now I must run, for if I leave it any longer I shan't have the courage to die. I am David. Amen.'

The dog kept nudging him. It wanted them to go back the way they had come, away from the spot where it sensed danger lurking.

'No,' David whispered, 'we can't go back – it's too late. You must keep still, King; and when they've hit me, perhaps you can get away by yourself.'

The dog licked his cheek eagerly, impatiently nudging him again and moving restlessly as if it wanted to get up. It nudged him once more – and then jumped up before David could stop it.

In one swift second David understood what the dog wanted. It did not run back the way they had come. It was a sheepdog and it had sensed danger... It was going to take David's place!

Barking loudly it sprang towards the men in the dark.

'Run!' something inside him told David. 'Run... run!' That was what the dog wanted him to do.

So he ran. He hesitated a moment and then ran more quickly than he had ever run in all his life. As he ran, he heard the men shouting and running too, but in a different direction... One of them yelled with pain – then came the sound of a shot and a strange loud bark from the dog.

David knew the dog was dead.

He went on running. He was some distance away now, and they had not heard him. But he ran on until he had left far behind the field where they had left the road an hour before. Then he threw himself down in a ditch sobbing, and gasping painfully for breath.

He felt as if he would never be able to stop crying, never. God of the pastures and waters, so strong that he could influence a person's thoughts, had let the dog run forward, although he knew it would be shot.

'Oh, you shouldn't have done it!' David sobbed again and again. 'The dog followed me, and I was never able to look after it properly. I couldn't even give it enough to eat and it had to steal to get food. The dog came with me of its own free will, and then had to die because of it...'

But then David suddenly realized he was wrong. It was not because it had followed him that the dog was dead. The dog had gone with him freely, and it had met its death freely, in order to protect David from *them*. It was a sheepdog, and it knew what it was doing. It had shown David what it wanted him to do, and then it had diverted the danger from him and faced it itself because it wanted to.

Its very bark as it sprang forward had seemed to say, 'Run, run!' And all the while David was running, he had known he must not turn back and try to save it. He must not let the dog's action be in vain.

A Life for A Life

PEGGY HEWITT

Jamie sat on an upturned herring crate, holding the cardboard box carefully on his knee. Around him the harbour was alive with cranes unloading the mackerel from the deep holds of the trawlers and dropping them into ice-packed boxes on the waiting lorries. Nets were being folded, yard upon yard of coarse black mesh edged with vivid pink floats that jostled each other in the folding machine, then fell into neat piles on the deck. Small boats darted across the water like flies on a mill pond and in the middle of the loch the foreign ships waited, slightly apart, to buy fish from the Scottish trawlers. Seagulls swooped and glided, eager for the odd fish that escaped the ice boxes, whilst others perched arrogantly on riggings and lobster pots.

Normally Jamie would have been excited by these familiar sights and sounds of the busy harbour, but today all he could think about was the cardboard box on his knees. In it, lying on a bed of straw, was McNab. McNab, who hadn't moved or opened his eyes since that great bully, Willie McDonald, after holding him aloft by his long soft ears, had dropped him, accidentally, onto the hard paving stones of Jamie's backyard. The little rabbit had lain there, not moving, and Jamie, after a moment's horror, had raced to find a box and some straw.

The vet. That was it. He must take McNab to the vet. But the vet lived across the loch at Aultnaharrie.

Gently he had lifted the limp little body onto the bed of straw and after shouting through to his mother that he would be late for tea he had set off for the harbour, followed at a distance by his friends Donald and Sandy. For to get to the vet they must take the ferry across Loch Broom.

They arrived at the harbour when the ferry was just about to set off. There was just room for one more, and Jamie clambered aboard. Then at the last minute the doctor arrived, anxious to get to a patient on the other side of the loch. Jamie had to give up his place and wait for the next trip.

So he sat there on the jetty, deaf and blind to what was going on around him, anger and anxiety battling in his heart. Anger against that unknown patient who had cost him his seat on the ferry, anxiety for McNab, lying so still on his bed of straw. They could have been there by now, safe at the vet's. Instead they were still waiting. Donald and Sandy stood close by, wishing they could help but not knowing what to do.

At last the boat returned and Jamie, with McNab, Donald and Sandy, clambered aboard. Then they had to wait, again, until it was time for the boat to leave. 'Will it never go?' Jamie thought.

At last the engine roared, the whole boat shuddered, and with a steady throbbing they were away. Away from the harbour and the trawlers, past the factory ships, approaching Aultnaharrie – painfully slowly. The seagulls that followed the ferry settled on the rocks as the boat was tied up. Jamie, carefully carrying his box, walked along the wooden jetty and across the shore to the vet's house. Donald and Sandy followed, but they waited by the gate as Jamie went inside.

Stillness settled on Aultnaharrie. Even the seagulls seemed to doze on the warm rocks, until the sound of the ferryboat starting its engine roused them to follow it once more back across the loch.

Jamie came out of the vet's house at last. His face was set and white, and he still carried the box. He passed Sandy and Donald without a word and went to sit on the jetty, waiting for the ferry to return once more. They hesitated, then went to sit by him; McNab was dead.

The ferry came back and, just as it was about to leave, a man came hurrying down the jetty. It was the doctor, returning from his visit. The ferryman waited for him to climb into the boat, then started the engine.

'Only just made it, eh Jamie,' the doctor said. Jamie just looked at him and the tears began to run down his cheeks.

'Who was it this time, doctor?' asked the ferryman, shouting above the noise of the engine.

'Old Bob Chisholm. He's been living on his own too long, I'm afraid,'

'Old Bob. He's been pushing his luck for years. Don't know where he puts all that beer he drinks, and that's the truth.'

'He had a heart attack this morning,' said the doctor briefly.

Their words drifted clearly down to Jamie, sitting in the stern of the boat, and the emptiness inside him suddenly filled with hot anger. His knuckles showed white through the brown of his hands and tears clogged his eyes.

'The doctor took my seat... I had to wait... and all for that drunken old man McNab is dead.' At that moment Jamie hated, really hated, for the first time in his life.

They were in the middle of the loch now, and as the boat turned to bring itself in line with the harbour mouth the lashing of the water against the sides matched the anger inside Jamie.

'Dear God, please let him die. He doesn't deserve to live. He's only wasted his life anyway, that old Bob Chisholm.' The seagulls dipped and hovered, carried on the slight breeze, and Jamie's thoughts echoed round and round in his head.

Then they were in calm water and another thought came to him.

'If old Bob dies – why – it will all have been for nothing, *all* have been wasted.' McNab was gone, nothing could alter that. But they'd had to wait at the harbour so that the doctor could come across to see old Bob. It had to be one or the other – it couldn't be both, or McNab had died for nothing.

They were tying up to the jetty now. Donald and Sandy were almost half way up the stone steps, and the doctor followed them, after a last brief word with the ferryman.

'See you again tonight, then.' And the ferryman nodded as the engine finally spluttered and was silent. He helped Jamie out of the boat with his box and watched him catch up with the doctor.

'You'll not let old Bob die, will you?' Jamie said quietly. 'He mustn't die.' The doctor looked at the anxious figure in front of him and smiled, very gently.

'Oh, old Bob's a tough bird. He'll be fine, just you see.'

'It's McNab, you see, he's...' The doctor nodded, understanding, smiled again at Jamie, then hurried away.

Jamie stood for a moment, thinking, then he kicked an old can into the water, hard, and walked over to where Donald and Sandy were waiting for him.

6
The Big Surprise

The day Jesus died was the worst day ever for his friends and followers. He'd told them they would see him again. But they didn't believe him. No one comes back to life once they're dead. So when Easter Sunday came, they had the biggest surprise of their lives. Bob Hartman's wonderful *Angel of Death and Life* gets right to the heart of the Easter story. *The Interview* puts Mary Magdalene in front of the microphone. *Deeper Magic* continues the story of Aslan. Then Haffertee Hamster makes another appearance; there's a story from Africa, and Susan Hill tells a story that features the old custom of decorating the graves with flowers at Easter.

Alive From the Dead!

From *The Lion Children's Bible*

PAT ALEXANDER

This story comes from the four New Testament Gospels.

It was Sunday morning, just before dawn. Everything was still. Then, as the first light touched the sky, the ground trembled and shook. An angel came and rolled away the stone that sealed Jesus' tomb. The guards were so frightened, they ran off.

When the women came, bringing their spices, the grave was open and the body had gone. The angel spoke to them:

'Don't be afraid,' he said. 'I know you are looking for Jesus. But he's not here. He's alive from the dead! Look, this is where his body was. Hurry and tell his friends. You will see him again soon.'

Jesus' friends refused to believe the women's story. They thought they were imagining things! But Peter and John went to the grave, to see for themselves.

John ran faster than Peter, and got there first. He looked inside the grave, but didn't go in. Then Peter arrived and they both went in.

They saw the cloths which had bound the body, lying untouched, with the cloth that had wrapped Jesus' head just a neck-space away. John knew at once that no one could have stolen the body. What the women had said was true! Jesus *was* alive from the dead!

The two men went home. But Mary Magdalene, who had followed them, stayed. She stood there, crying. She could not understand what had happened. Then she caught sight of a man she thought was the gardener.

'If you have taken him away,' she said, 'please tell me where to find him.' She did not know she was talking to Jesus!

Then Jesus said, 'Mary!' She knew at once who it was. Joy flooded through her.

'Tell my friends you have seen me,' Jesus said.

Later that day, a man called Cleopas and another of Jesus'

followers were walking home to Emmaus, outside Jerusalem. As they were talking, a stranger caught up with them.

'Why are you so sad?' he asked.

'Are you the only person in Jerusalem who doesn't know what's been happening there these last few days?' Cleopas answered.

'Why, what's that?' he asked.

'About Jesus of Nazareth,' Cleopas replied. 'He was a great teacher. We all thought he was God's promised King. But they put him to death on Friday. Then this morning some women went to his grave. They said the body had gone, and that an angel had told them Jesus was alive!'

'Why are you so puzzled?' the stranger asked. 'Don't you know that the prophets said all this would happen?' And he began to explain.

When they got home, they asked him in.

'It's nearly dark. Come and have a meal with us.'

When the meal was ready, the visitor took the bread in his hands and thanked God for it. Then they knew that the stranger was Jesus – and no sooner did they recognize him, than he had gone.

In great excitement they hurried back to Jerusalem to tell their friends.

The followers were all together, with other friends of Jesus. 'It *must* be true,' they said. 'Peter has seen him, too.'

The doors were locked. They were afraid. Suddenly, there was Jesus, standing in the room with them! They were terrified at first. They thought they were seeing a ghost! But Jesus calmed them down. He showed them the marks of the nails in his hands and feet. Then they knew it must be him.

'Touch me,' he said. 'Ghosts aren't made of flesh and bones.' Then they knew he was real.

Still they could hardly believe it was true. It was so good to see and talk to him again!

'Is there anything to eat?' Jesus asked.

They gave him some fish and watched him eat it. After that there were no more doubts. It *was* Jesus. He was real. He was alive!

Jesus explained how all that had happened was part of God's wonderful plan. He quoted from God's law, from the prophets and the psalms.

'God's King had to suffer and die,' he said, 'and live again. The penalty for sin has been paid. Death has been conquered. Now God offers a free pardon to everyone who believes and comes to him for new life. It's good news for people of every nation. And you will go and tell them.'

'Butterfly'

JOYCE KILMER

Waken, sleeping butterfly,
Burst your chrysalis prison.
Spread your beauteous wings and fly,
Christ, the Lord is risen.

Angel of Death and Life

From *Angels, Angels, All Around*

BOB HARTMAN

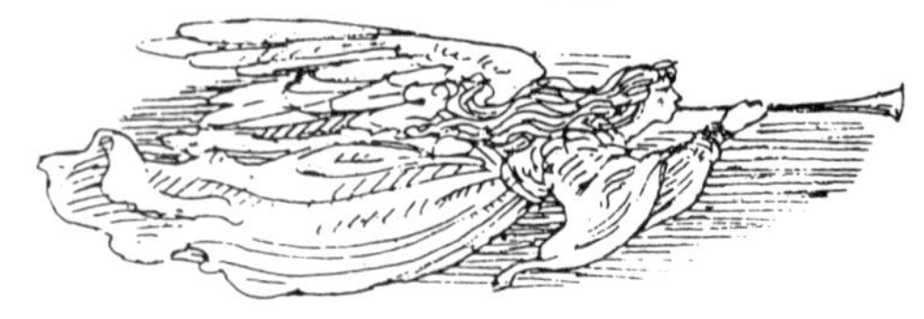

The angel sat in the dark and waited.

This was the most unusual assignment he had ever received. Up till now, his missions had always been straightforward – keeping children from falling into wells, helping lost travellers find their way. Typical guardian angel kind of stuff.

But this job was different, very different. A quick beam of light to mark the location, and a strange set of orders that simply said he should wait for his partner to arrive. Partner? He'd never had a partner before. He was big and strong and could do most things on his own. So he couldn't help wondering what this was all about.

And then the angel saw something.

The sun reached one long finger over the horizon and, sure enough, there was someone coming towards him, wading slowly through the darkness as if it were a thick, black sea. Could this be his partner? If so, it was the most unusual angel he had ever seen.

No song. No shimmer. No shine. There was hardly a hint of heaven about him. Instead, he was thin and tired – a small grey mouse of an angel. Barely an angel at all, it seemed.

The first angel raised his hand in a greeting. 'Hello,' he said. 'My name is Candriel. Who are you?'

The second angel sat down beside his partner, but it was a minute or two before he spoke. And when he did, it was in a mouse's whisper that matched his looks.

'My name is Destroyer,' he said solemnly. 'I am the Angel of Death.'

An early morning breeze blew past the angels, but it was not the breeze that made Candriel shiver. He'd heard of this angel. Everyone had. How he'd killed Egyptian first-borns and set God's people free. How he'd slain, single-handed, 185,000 Assyrian soldiers in one night. But to look at him now, sitting there all small and grey and quiet, it hardly seemed possible.

Could this really be the Angel of Death? Candriel wondered.

And what kind of mission was this going to be?

'I suppose you have the orders?' said Candriel uncertainly.

The Angel of Death nodded and laid a bony hand on one of his pockets. 'I do,' he sighed. 'But I was told not to open them until we saw women coming up the hill. It's got something to do with a secret – a surprise.'

A partner. A signal. A surprise. This job gets stranger and stranger, thought Candriel. But all he dared say was, 'What do you suppose the orders are?'

The Angel of Death shook his head. 'Oh, that's not hard to guess. All you have to do is look around.'

The sun's bright scalp edged over the horizon, and Candriel looked. They were in the middle of a graveyard.

'Death again,' Destroyer sighed. 'Seems like death is always part of the job for me. So I guess it makes sense that I should play some part in this death, too. The saddest death of all.'

Candriel looked again. The sun was a little higher now, and he could see it all clearly. The garden graveyard. The sleeping soldiers. The city of Jerusalem off in the distance. The huge stone that sealed the tomb beneath them.

'So you've guessed who's in the tomb we're sitting on,' said Destroyer.

'Jesus,' whispered Candriel. 'It's Jesus, isn't it? It's God's Son.'

A soldier grunted in his sleep. A bird whistled in the distance. And the Angel of Death just nodded.

'I saw it happen, you know,' said Candriel after a while. 'I saw him die on the cross. Our whole battalion was ready to burst through the sky, beat the stuffing out of those soldiers, and save him. Uproot that cross, tear it right out of the ground – that's what I would have done. But they wouldn't let us do anything. They said the signal had to come from Him. And the signal never came.'

Destroyer turned a grey face to his partner. 'I didn't watch,' he said softly. 'I couldn't. I've seen too much death already. I'm sure He had a reason. He must have. But that didn't make it any easier. Didn't ease the terrible hurt.'

'No,' agreed Candriel. 'He suffered a lot. You could see that. They did some awful things to him.'

'That's not what I mean,' said Destroyer. 'I mean the other kind of hurt that comes with death. Saying goodbye to your friends, to the ones you love. They say that even his mother was there.'

Candriel said nothing. He looked puzzled.

'You're a guardian angel, aren't you?' asked Destroyer. But it wasn't really a question. 'Big and strong – the rescuing type.'

'Right,' said Candriel. 'And I'm good at what I do.'

'I'm sure you are,' said the Angel of Death. 'And I'm also sure you feel a lot of joy and gratitude from the people you rescue.'

'Oh, yes!' Candriel smiled.

'Well, it's different when you're the Angel of Death. Take the Assyrian army, for example. They had the city of Jerusalem surrounded. They were going to slaughter most of God's people and make slaves of the rest. It was my job to stop them.'

'That must have been difficult,' Candriel interrupted, 'to kill so many of them. I mean, with you being so small.'

The Angel of Death looked up at his partner and slowly shook his head. 'No,' he sighed. 'Doing the job was the easy part. A quick breath in the face. That's all it took. Then their eyes glazed over and their hearts grew still.

'The hard part was the thoughts – those thousands and thousands of sad goodbye thoughts:

My wife... I'll never see you again.
I'm sorry, Mother. I promised you I would come back.
Grow up well, my son... I will miss you.

'Missing. Death is all about missing. That's what I remember most about that night. And that's what I think must have been so hard for Jesus and his friends.'

Candriel looked at his partner. And what he saw was sadness. Sadness like some great thick shell that seemed to crush and shrink Destroyer.

'I just wish,' the Angel of Death concluded, 'I just wish that once I could have a mission where I remembered not sadness and loss, but the kind of joy and gratitude that you have felt so often.'

Candriel didn't know what to say. But he was a guardian angel, after all. So at least he knew what to do. He opened up one shining silver wing, and reaching through the sadness, he wrapped it around the Angel of Death.

They sat there together in the sadness and the new day's light. And then Candriel spotted the women.

'That's the signal,' he said. 'It's time to read our orders.'

The Angel of Death reached into his pocket and handed the scroll to his partner. 'You read it,' he said.

Candriel took the scroll and started to unroll it. 'It's probably very simple,' he said. 'The women are coming.'

'They're friends of Jesus. We're probably supposed to protect them from these soldiers. It's going to be all right. You'll see.'

And then he read the scroll out loud.

'Candriel,' the orders said. 'Guardian Angel, kind and strong: you wanted so badly to free my Son from his cross. But that was not within your power. What is now within your power is to roll away the stone. Open his tomb and show the world that the one who died on the cross is now alive – free from death forever!

'As for you, Destroyer, faithful servant, Angel of Death: someone needs to tell these women that the one they miss is alive. Who better to share this joyful news than one who understands their sadness and loss?'

It took hardly a second. Candriel dropped the orders, leaped off the tomb, and rolled away the stone.

Destroyer was right behind, climbing down after him into the grave. It was empty.

It was empty!

And that's when Candriel saw his partner change.

The soldiers said it was an earthquake. They said they saw a flash of lightning. But Candriel knew different.

The sound that cracked the morning stillness was a sad whisper exploding into a shout of joy. And the light that stunned the soldiers was a grim, grey shadow bursting bright to white.

'He's not in here. He is risen! He is alive!' Destroyer shouted to the women.

And the Angel of Death became, forevermore, the Angel of Life.

‘E is for Easter’

RACHEL HARTLEY

E is for Easter, coming again soon,
A is for angels near the tomb,
S is for stone which was rolled away
T is for tomb found empty that day,
E is for early morning, the women are glad,
R is for the Risen Lord, no need to be sad.

The Interview

From *The Davidson Affair*

STUART JACKMAN

The news-wire which reaches the studio reads: 'Jesus Davidson, executed for treason Friday, reported seen in city early this morning.' So Cass Tennel is sent post-haste to Jerusalem to investigate for a TV documentary. Mary Magdalene – 'Miss Magdala' – is an obvious subject for his interview...

'I wonder if you could tell us what happened, Miss Magdala? At the tomb, I mean.'

'He broke out. Nothing they could do could hold him.' She laughed, spreading her hands in a gesture of excitement. 'They sealed up the tomb, you know, and mounted a guard. It was ridiculous. Pathetic. Like tying up a sleeping lion with cotton thread. When he wakened he just snapped the thread and strode out...'

'You say you saw him there, outside the tomb?'

'I did indeed.'

'Alive?'

'Of course.'

'Miss Magdala,' I said brutally. 'I'm sorry, but that's just not possible.'

She was quite unshaken. 'It's a miracle, Mr Tennel. They come naturally to him, of course. I'm ashamed to think how slow we've been to recognize this.'

'It's understandable,' I said. 'I'm not much for miracles myself.'

'He performed many, Mr Tennel. A great many.'

'So I'm told.'

'The trouble is, people misunderstood them.'

'Didn't believe in them, you mean?'

'Oh no. They believed all right. If you see a cripple get up and walk, and listen to a deaf-mute you've known all your life suddenly start singing, you haven't much option, have you? When it happens like that, in front of a crowd, you've got to believe it.' She shook her head again – that gesture of mingled frustration and excitement I was beginning to associate with people who had known Davidson. 'It was the meaning of what he did they couldn't understand. They thought he was just a man doing something extraordinary.'

'Yes,' I said.

'No. That's exactly the point. He wasn't an ordinary man. He was God. God in person, doing the things that came naturally to him. People always said, "How can this village nobody work miracles?" But the real question is, "How can God walk about Israel like a man?" That's the basic miracle, Mr Tennel, that he was here at all. Once you've seen that, the rest is perfectly logical.'

'Even a resurrection?'

'Especially that. Death can't hold God…'

I said, 'And you saw him there, in the garden outside the tomb?'

'That's right. I saw him and talked to him…'

I said, 'How did you come to be in the garden so early in the morning? Was it pre-arranged before he died? A sort of rendezvous?'

She laughed. 'Nothing so dramatic. It was simply our first opportunity to visit his tomb. We have a strict rule about not working on the Sabbath, as I expect you know. We had to wait until first light yesterday before we could go.'

'Yes, but why did you go? Was it just a sentimental journey?'

'In a way, I suppose it was,' she said frankly. 'But practical too. We took spices and ointment and – oh, it sounds absurd now, a bunch of women in heavy mourning going to preserve a corpse. But it was all we could think of doing. We'd had to stand by and watch them take him away and kill him. And the burial on Friday was very rushed. We had to get finished before the Sabbath started at sunset. Yesterday morning we decided to do things properly. Give him a decent burial at least.' She smiled. 'I expect it all sounds very odd to you, Mr Tennel. But our Jewish funeral customs are important to us.'

'I understand,' I said.

'We were terribly worried about how we were going to get into the tomb – what with that great stone slab sealing the entrance and the guard there and everything. But of course, when we got there, the guards had gone and the tomb was wide open. And when we looked inside, it was empty.'

I nodded. This was familiar ground by now. 'You've considered the possibility of grave-robbers?'

'It was our first thought. I remember Salome – she was one of the group – saying in that rather acid voice she puts on when she's upset, "Even when the poor soul's dead they can't leave him in peace..."

'But it wasn't that at all, of course,' she said. 'We rushed back to the house and told the men. And John Zebedee and Peter Johnson went back straightaway to see for themselves. I followed behind but I hadn't a hope of catching up with them.'

I said, 'I'd like to get this quite right. It's important, I think. Are you in fact saying that the men were surprised at your news of the empty tomb?'

'And angry. Peter especially. I've never seen him so wild.'

'It would be true to say, then, that these men who were his closest friends never expected him to come back from the dead?'

'None of us did, Mr Tennel. None of us.'

'Although he had on several occasions promised to do just that?'

'In spite of that we didn't expect to see him alive again. I'm ashamed to have to say it, but it's true.'

'And the men had been with you right through from Friday evening?'

'Yes.'

'Thank you,' I said. 'Please go on. What happened when you got to the tomb the second time?'

'I saw Peter coming out. I hardly recognized him, he looked so old and beaten. John took his arm and they went off together, walking slowly. They passed right by me but I don't think either of them knew I was there. They were like men walking in their sleep.'

'And did you go after them?'

'No. I stayed on. I don't know why. I was weeping and terribly upset, and...'

'I quite understand, Miss Magdala. This has all been a tremendous strain on you.'

She looked at me steadily and said, 'You don't believe it, do you? You don't believe he's alive again?'

'I'm open to conviction,' I said.

She shook her head. 'You think I'm not quite myself. A little bit off-centre. You think it's all been too much of a shock for me. Well, it was a shock, finding that empty tomb. A terrible shock.'

'Yes,' I said. 'Of course.'

'The thought of them mauling him about. Dragging him out of his grave in the middle of the night and digging a hole somewhere and dropping his body in and stamping the ground down on top of him. Just for a moment or two, there by myself in the garden when the men had gone, I thought I was going out of my mind.' She smiled, a warm, sane smile. 'And then he came and spoke to me.'

'Jesus Davidson? You're sure?'

'Yes. He was suddenly there and he asked me why I was crying. He sounded so – so normal and relaxed I didn't think it was him at first. Funny isn't it, the way a familiar voice sounds strange when you don't expect to hear it? But then he spoke my name. "Mary" he said. And I knew who he was.'

'An Easter Carol'

CHRISTINA ROSSETTI

Spring bursts today,
For Christ is risen and all the earth's at play.

Flash forth, thou sun,
The rain is over and gone, its work is done.

Winter is past,
Sweet spring is come at last, is come at last.

Bud, fig and vine,
Bud, olive, fat with fruit and oil, and wine.

Break forth this morn
In roses, thou but yesterday a thorn.

Uplift thy head,
O pure white lily through the winter dead.

Beside your dams
Leap and rejoice, you merry-making lambs.

All herds and flocks
Rejoice, all beasts of thickets and of rocks.

Sing, creatures, sing,
Angels and men and birds, and everything...

Deeper Magic

From *The Lion, the Witch and the Wardrobe*

C.S. LEWIS

The Lion Aslan has given himself up to the White Witch, to save the life of Edmund and all Narnia. On the Stone Table, she has put him to death. Susan and Lucy, Edmund's sisters, have secretly watched it all, in horror. At last the Witch and her followers move away…

Susan and Lucy crept out into the open hill-top. The moon was getting low and thin clouds were passing across her, but still they could see the shape of the Lion lying dead in his bonds. And down they both knelt in the wet grass and kissed his cold face and stroked his beautiful fur – what was left of it – and cried till they could cry no more. And then they looked at each other and held each other's hands for mere loneliness and cried again; and then again were silent. At last Lucy said, 'I can't bear to look at that horrible muzzle. I wonder, could we take it off?'

So they tried. And after a lot of working at it (for their fingers were cold and it was now the darkest part of the night) they succeeded. And when they saw his face without it they burst out crying again and kissed it and fondled it and wiped away the blood and the foam as well as they could. And it was all more lonely and hopeless and horrid than I know how to describe.

'I wonder could we untie him as well?' said Susan presently. But the enemies, out of pure spitefulness, had drawn the cords so tight that the girls could make nothing of the knots.

I hope no one who reads this book has been quite as miserable as Susan and Lucy were that night; but if you have been – if you've been up all night and cried till you have no more tears left in you – you will know that there comes in the end a sort of quietness. You feel as if nothing was ever going to happen again. At any rate that was how it felt to these two. Hours and hours seemed to go by in this dead calm, and they hardly noticed that they were getting colder and colder. But at last Lucy noticed two other things. One was that the sky on the east side of the hill was a little less dark than it had been an hour ago. The other was some tiny movement going on in the grass at her feet. At first she took no interest in this. What did it matter? Nothing mattered now! But at last she saw that whatever-it-was had begun to move up the upright stones of the Stone Table. And now whatever-they-were were moving about on Aslan's body. She peered closer. They were little grey things.

'Ugh!' said Susan from the other side of the Table. 'How beastly! There are horrid little mice crawling over him. Go away, you little beasts.' And she raised her hand to frighten them away.

'Wait!' said Lucy, who had been looking at them more closely still. 'Can you see what they're doing?'

Both girls bent down and stared.

'I do believe – ' said Susan. 'But how queer! They're nibbling away at the cords!'

'That's what I thought,' said Lucy. 'I think they're friendly mice. Poor little things – they don't realize he's dead. They think it'll do some good untying him.'

It was quite definitely lighter by now. Each of the girls noticed for the first time the white face of the other. They could see the mice nibbling away; dozens and dozens, even hundreds, of little field mice. And at last, one by one, the ropes were all gnawed through.

The sky in the east was whitish by now and the stars were getting fainter – all except one very big one low down on the eastern horizon. They felt colder than they had been all night. The mice crept away again.

The girls cleared away the remains of the gnawed ropes. Aslan looked more like himself without them. Every moment his dead face looked nobler, as the light grew and they could see it better.

In the wood behind them a bird gave a chuckling sound. It had been so still for hours and hours that it startled them. Then another bird answered it. Soon there were birds singing all over the place.

It was quite definitely early morning now, not late night.

'I'm so cold,' said Lucy.

'So am I,' said Susan. 'Let's walk about a bit…'

At last… the red turned to gold along the line where the sea and the sky met and very slowly up came the edge of the sun.

At that moment they heard from behind them a loud noise – a great cracking, deafening noise as if a giant had broken a giant's plate.

'What's that?' said Lucy, clutching Susan's arm.

'I – I feel afraid to turn round,' said Susan; 'something awful is happening.'

'They're doing something worse to *Him*,' said Lucy, 'Come on!' And she turned, pulling Susan round with her.

The rising of the sun had made everything look so different – all the colours and shadows were changed – that for a moment they didn't see the important thing. Then they did. The Stone Table was broken into two pieces by a great crack that ran down it from end to end; and there was no Aslan.

'Oh, oh, oh!' cried the two girls, rushing back to the Table.

'Oh, it's *too* bad,' sobbed Lucy; 'they might have left the body alone.'

'Who's done it?' cried Susan. 'What does it mean? Is it more magic?'

'Yes!' said a great voice behind their backs. 'It is more magic.' They looked round. There, shining in the sunrise, larger than they had seen him before, shaking his mane (for it had apparently grown again) stood Aslan himself.

'Oh, Aslan!' cried both the children, staring up at him, almost as much frightened as they were glad.

'Aren't you dead then, dear Aslan?' said Lucy.

'Not now,' said Aslan.

'You're not – not a – ?' asked Susan in a shaky voice. She couldn't bring herself to say the word *ghost*. Aslan stooped his golden head and licked her forehead. The warmth of his breath and a rich sort of smell that seemed to hang about his hair came all over her.

'Do I look it?' he said.

'Oh, you're real, you're real! Oh, Aslan!' cried Lucy, and both girls flung themselves upon him and covered him with kisses.

'But what does it all mean?' asked Susan when they were somewhat calmer.

'It means,' said Aslan, 'that though the Witch knew the Deep Magic, there is a magic deeper still which she did not know. Her knowledge goes back only to the dawn of time. But if she could have looked a little further back, into the stillness and the darkness before Time dawned, she would have read there a different incantation. She would have known that when a willing victim who had committed no treachery was killed in a traitor's stead, the Table would crack and Death itself would start working backwards.'

Pieces of Howl

From *Haffertee's First Easter*

JANET AND JOHN PERKINS

Haffertee, the soft-toy hamster who belongs to Diamond Yo, is busy finding out all about Easter when his great friend Howl Owl goes missing...

Something was very wrong.

Haffertee had a strange feeling inside.

He couldn't think what it was at first but then all at once he knew.

Howl Owl was missing!...

He wasn't anywhere around the house. The shelf above the door in Yo's room was empty...

There was no sign of Howl Owl at the top of the garden, so Haffertee decided to go and look in the wilderness.

He found William the donkey up there, on the grassy patch under the beech tree.

'Hee Haw Hallo!' he called, when he saw Haffertee coming. 'How are you?'

'Very well, thank you,' said Haffertee, as cheerfully as he could. He wasn't really feeling very well at all. There was a sick hollow in his tummy.

'Have you seen Howl Owl at all this morning?' he asked politely.

William nodded his head towards a path that led up the hill to an old ruined cottage.

'I saw him very early this morning, skimming along up there,' he said.

Haffertee was beginning to get very anxious and he set off quickly up the path without even saying thank you.

William didn't seem to notice. He returned to crunching thistles.

The path beyond the grassy patch was all new to Haffertee. He hadn't been that way before and it did look rather frightening. He gritted his teeth, swallowed a fear or two, and hurried on. He wanted to find Howl Owl.

What he found up there in the ruined cottage was very, very sad.

He found... not Howl, but *pieces* of Howl.

His wings were under a stone.

His body was dangling from a broken shelf.

And his stuffing was all over the place.

There could be no doubt about it.

Howl Owl was dead.

Haffertee just stood there and sobbed. He had never seen anything like it. Who could have done such a cruel thing?

Haffertee did not know. All he knew was that his dear, dear friend Howl Owl was dead.

At last, when there were no more sobs left, he collected all the bits of his friend together and half-carried, half-dragged them down the hill, past William, through the bramble tunnel, round past the nettle patch, through the hole in the fence and down the garden steps to Hillside House.

He was tired out when he got to the back door.

He knocked wearily.

Diamond Yo opened the door.

When she saw Haffertee and the pieces of Howl she let out a loud cry and the tears began to run down her cheeks on to her green dress.

She lifted Haffertee up with the pieces of Howl and held them both very close.

Ma Diamond suddenly appeared from the kitchen.

'Whatever is the matter?' she asked. 'Why are you crying?'

Then she saw the pieces of Howl.

'Oh!' was all she could say.

Slowly and sadly the three of them walked upstairs to Diamond Yo's room. They put the terrible bundle of torn Howl on to the bed and just sat there together.

Haffertee said nothing.

Diamond Yo said nothing.

Ma Diamond said nothing.

There was just nothing to say.

Life in the Diamond family would never be the same again.

It was a very sad Haffertee and Diamond Yo who went to bed that night. God didn't seem to be very nice at all. They didn't say any prayers.

Neither of them slept much, either.

They just lay there, thinking about the wonderful times they had had together with Howl Owl.

Morning came slowly and smiled at them through the curtains. Saturday always seemed to come in smiling.

But there was no one on the shelf above the door.

'Good morning, Haffertee! Good morning, Yo!' said a surprisingly cheerful voice. 'Look what I've got!'

The two of them turned round slowly – and looked.

Then they both shot out of bed.

They simply could not believe their eyes.

There was Ma Diamond holding a very familiar figure in her arms. It was Howl Owl.

He was all put together again.

His eyes were bright and shining and his black beak was gleaming. He was as fat as ever. He was alive and real and himself again.

Haffertee and Diamond Yo were absolutely amazed and delighted.

'However did you do it?' asked Diamond Yo.

'Yes,' chirped Haffertee cheekily. 'However did you do it?'

'Weller…' said Ma Diamond in a deep voice, trying to sound like Howl Owl, and smiling merrily.

'Weller… I made him in the first place, didn't I? So I made him again. I spent a lot of last night putting him all together again – and here he is!'

'Yes. Here I jolly well am,' said Howl Owl in his deepest voice ever. 'Here I jolly well am!'

'Oh Howl!' shouted Haffertee, with a lovely warm feeling coming up from his toes all the way to his ears. 'Oh Howl!'

He rushed over to his big barn owl friend and hugged him as tight as he could. (It wasn't very tight, because Howl was so far round.) Howl lifted one of his wings and rested it gently on Haffertee's shoulders.

They stood there together for a long time.

Everything was all right again now.

Ma Diamond had worked a miracle!

'The Colour of Easter'

CORAL RUMBLE

What is the colour of Easter?
What is the shade of its name?
Is it yellow like chicks
And like daffodils
Or red like the colour of pain?

What is the colour of Easter?
What is the shade of its name?
Is it white like a lamb
And a spring-cloud
Or black like the colour of shame?

What is the colour of Easter?
What is the shade of its name?
Is it brown like decay
And old photos
Or gold like the colour of grain?

Excitement at Easter

A story from Africa

WENDY GREEN

Rudo could hardly sleep. It wasn't the leopards growling in the bush that surrounded the school keeping her awake. It wasn't the monkeys chattering. It wasn't even the other girls in the same bedroom. She was just so excited. Tomorrow was Easter Sunday and Easter was the time that she liked best in all the year.

The music group had been busy rehearsing Easter songs for weeks. Rudo loved to listen to the beat of the drums and watch the streamers waving as the timbrels swooped and soared making multi-coloured patterns.

Nobody was supposed to see the rehearsals for the Easter play but little groups had been practising in corners whenever there was a spare moment.

This year the children in Rudo's class had been part of the crowd who waved branches and shouted 'Hosanna' when Jesus rode into Jerusalem. Rudo's best friend had acted the part of the man who owned the donkey.

Two of the girls in the top class pretended to be the donkey. It must have been very hot and stuffy under the big grey blanket they had thrown over their backs but judging by the giggles during rehearsals they didn't seem to mind too much.

Everyone in Rudo's class liked the girl who had been chosen to play Jesus. She always had time for the little ones. She didn't shout or tell them to go away, even when she had a lot of studying to do.

Nobody wanted to play Judas, the wicked man who had sold Jesus for thirty pieces of silver. Teacher had tried to explain to them that it had to be. She'd said that if Jesus hadn't died we would never have known how much God loves us. Rudo was glad that God cared so much but still felt sad to think of Jesus dying.

Lots of her friends felt the same. On Good Friday everyone had been very quiet and thoughtful. No one ran around or shouted. They had been thinking of Jesus on the cross with the crown of thorns on his head. There were thorn bushes outside the school grounds. Rudo had trodden on a thorn one day and it had hurt very much.

All the children had been glad when Saturday came. In the morning there had been the usual work to do around the grounds. Everywhere had to be clean and smart for Sunday, especially Easter Sunday. Then they'd had games and activities, and at last, the Easter play. Rudo and her friends had shouted as loud as they could, and the donkey had managed not to giggle with so many people watching.

Rudo yawned. It had been a long day. There had been so much to see and do. Now she must go to sleep. They had to get up early in the morning, before it was really light. Just like the women who went to visit Jesus' grave on the first Easter Sunday. Those women were sad too, because their friend Jesus was dead.

Rudo smiled in the darkness. She knew the next bit of the story. It didn't end there. She snuggled under the covers and closed her eyes.

The next thing she knew someone was shaking her, and shouting, 'Wake up. Wake up.' Rudo stretched and blinked. It was morning. Easter morning. She jumped out of bed. 'Wake up,' she called excitedly, shaking the girl in the next bed. 'It's Easter. Jesus is risen.'

The sounds echoed from hut to hut. Soon all the children and teachers were out of bed.

As quickly as they could they made their way to a rocky hillside outside the village shouting and singing, 'Hosanna. Hallelujah. Makabongwe.'

The stone had been rolled away from the grave. They could shout and dance and sing. There was no need to be sad any more. Jesus was not dead. He was alive, and with his people always, not only on Easter Sunday.

'Easter'

WENDY GREEN

Birds nesting
Grass growing
Leaves budding
Wind blowing

Soldiers marching
Jesus dying
Peter sobbing
Mary crying

Sunday dawning
Jesus living
Friends running
No more grieving.

On Easter Day

From *In the Springtime of the Year*

SUSAN HILL

When Ruth's young husband, Ben, is killed in an accident she is frozen with grief. But time passes, Easter comes round, and she goes to the village church with Ben's younger brother, Jo...

The last time Ruth had been inside the church was for Ben's funeral. Well, she would not brood about that, it was over and she must think only about this day, trying to understand. And she must go in among all the people and never mind if they stared at her and judged her. But seeing them walking up the hill ahead, and a group standing in the church porch, she clenched her hands tightly, and it seemed that her heart would leap up into her mouth.

'Oh, Ruth, look! Look.'

They had reached the lych-gate. Jo was pointing. She looked.

Had she been blind last year? Had it looked like this? The churchyard was brilliant as a garden with the patterned flowers, almost every grave was decked out in growing white and blue, pink and butter-yellow, and underneath it all, the watery moss and the vivid grass; it was as though all the people had indeed truly risen and were dancing in the sunshine, there was nothing but rejoicing and release. She walked slowly across the turf to the side of the church and stood, looking towards Ben's grave. It was like a sunburst...

Stepping into the church was like stepping into some sunlit clearing of the woods; there were flowers and leaves and the scents of them everywhere, the altar and pulpit, the font and the rails were wound about with ropes of white and golden blossoms, the ledges were banked with bluebells on mounds of moss, and the sun shone in through the windows, sending rippling coloured lights on to the stone walls, catching fire on the brass of the cross and the lectern. Ruth felt nothing but happiness, she walked down between the high wooden pews right to the front of the church, and looked here and there and smiled, if she caught someone's eye, and did not mind that they seemed embarrassed, uncertain of her. She went into the same pew and for a second saw again how it had been that other day, with the long pale coffin that had seemed to fill the whole building, the whole world.

But what she became aware of after that was not the presence of the village people sitting or kneeling behind her, but of others, the church was full of all those who had ever prayed in it, the air was crammed and vibrating with their goodness and the freedom and power of their resurrection...

7
Eggs for Easter

Long before Christian times, eggs were exchanged to celebrate the new life that comes each springtime. But for Christians the egg, and the chick that hatches from it, makes a good picture of Jesus, alive again from the dark tomb. The custom of specially-decorated eggs for Easter spread far and wide. So my Easter story book would not be complete without a section on Easter eggs.

'Easter Eggs'

ANON (TRANSLATED FROM A TRADITIONAL RUSSIAN EASTER SONG)

Easter eggs! Easter eggs! Give to him that begs!
For Christ the Lord is arisen.

To the poor, open door, something give from your store!
For Christ the Lord is arisen.

Those who hoard can't afford, moth and rust their reward!
For Christ the Lord is arisen.

Eastertide, like a bride, comes, and won't be denied.
For Christ the Lord is arisen.

Consolation Prize

LAVINIA DERWENT

In the days when I was an Infant at the village school the one and only prize I ever won was for the best dyed egg. The presentation was made by none other than the man who wrote *Peter Pan*, Sir J.M. Barrie, who happened to be staying with friends in the district at the time. It should have been a proud occasion for me, but for one thing. I had not dyed the egg myself.

It was Jessie, the odd-job woman at the farm, who had done it for me by covering the egg with a piece of lace and putting an onion (only she called it an *ingan*) in the water to colour it.

Sir James was greatly impressed and declared that if all eggs looked like that he would have a boiled one for his breakfast every morning. To my shame he presented me with a book of Bible Stories. There was a picture of the Prodigal Son on the cover, and I ran breathlessly home to present it to Jessie, the rightful winner, but she handed it back to me and said, 'Hoots-toots, lassie, you read it yoursel'. Maybe it'll lairn ye a lesson.'

It did. Next year, to expiate my sins, I did the deed myself. Only better. I found an even lacier piece of lace, put *two* onions in the water to give it a richer hue, and dyed a couple of eggs to be on the safe side.

Perfect they were, both worthy of first prize, in my opinion. I swithered about which to take; the rose-patterned one, or the one with wee butterflies on it. It was impossible to choose, so I wrapped them both up in tissue paper and put them carefully in my schoolbag. Maybe I would get first *and* second prizes.

I had to stop at the old roadman's cottage, as I did every morning, to collect Wee Wullie. We all have our burdens to bear and Wullie was mine. He was a small sauchly* child, with his stockings hanging down and an unwashed, unkempt, neglected look about him. He lived a kind of hand-to-mouth existence with

* sallow

the old roadman, his grandfather, who was often ill and out of work, and seldom, I daresay, had a cooked meal. Though that never occurred to me at the time. I just thought of Wee Wullie as a nuisance. He was always trying to play truant and snivelling. 'I dinna want to be learnt!' But the teacher had told me I *must* bring him. So I had to act as sergeant-major.

'Come on, you!' I called out at the cottage door; and at last Wee Wullie came shuffling out with his laces trailing from his boots and his patched jersey on back to front. He walked a few paces behind me, like a lord-in-waiting, and I had to turn round every now and again to see that he had not jouked** me and done a dash over the fence.

'Where's your dyed egg?' I asked him.

'Haveny got one,' said Wullie, kicking his toes.

'What? Fancy not even bothering to dye an egg for the competition. Lazy thing!'

Outside Bella-the-Shop's door, I had a sudden tussle with myself. After all, I had *two* eggs.

'Here!' I said, fishing in my schoolbag. 'You can have one of mine.'

I did eenie-meenie-miny-mo and handed him one of the eggs wrapped up in its tissue paper. I left him clutching it, with his eyes sparkling, and went in to buy a new jotter. I had no money left over to buy sweets; but never mind! It was rumoured that Lady Somebody was coming to judge the dyed eggs and the first prize would be a big box of chocolates. But what if Wee Wullie won it?

He was still standing where I left him with the tissue paper clutched in his hand. But where was the egg?

'I've etten't,' he confessed, wiping his mouth.

'Etten't!' I cried, aghast at the enormity of his sin. When I saw bits of coloured shell scattered around him I raged, 'You're a wicked thing! What did you do that for?'

Wee Wullie began to blubber. 'I was h-hungry!'

Hungry! I stared at him in amazement. It had never entered my head that anyone could be so hungry that he would eat a prize-winning dyed egg. It was easy enough for me; the hens just laid them and I went to gather them.

'Stop greetin'***,' I said crossly. 'Come on; we'll be late.'

** dodged

*** crying

I had a fight with myself all the way to the school gate. The bell was ringing before I finally made my great sacrifice. 'Here! Have the other egg,' I said, thrusting it at Wullie. 'But you're not to eat it. It's for the prize.'

Lady Thing was a rotten judge. She gave Maggie Turnbull the box of chocolates, and Wee Wullie was not even in the first three. But at least she gave him a consolation prize. A bar of scented soap. Wee Wullie was as pleased as punch and sniffed at it all the way home. But it would have been better if he could have etten't.

There and then I decided that I would take an extra dinner-piece with me every day and share it with Wullie.

The Easter Egg

From *The Country Child*

ALISON UTTLEY

This story looks back to the early years of this century. Susan is an only child. She lives on a farm called Windystone Hall, and walks to the village school every day, through the Dark Wood. Tom and Margaret are Susan's father and mother, Mr and Mrs Garland. Becky helps in the house and Joshua works on the farm.

One morning Susan looked out of her window and saw that spring had really come...

She wrinkled her nose with pleasure and a rabbit with her little one directly below the window, on the steep slope, wrinkled her nose, too, as she sat up among the nettles and borage...

Susan... laughed at the rabbit, and then ran downstairs. It was Good Friday...

Her mother met her in the hall, running excitedly to call her. There was a parcel addressed to Mr, Mrs and Miss Garland. Susan had never been called Miss before, except by the old man at the village who said, 'You're late, Missie,' when she ran past his cottage on the way to school.

With trembling fingers Susan and Margaret untied the knots, for never, never had anyone at Windystone been so wasteful as to cut a piece of string.

Inside was a flower-embroidered table-cloth for Margaret, a book of the Christian Saints and Martyrs of the Church for Tom, which he took with wondering eyes, and a box containing six Easter eggs.

There were three chocolate eggs, covered with silver paper, a wooden egg painted with pictures round the edge, a red egg with a snake inside, and a beautiful pale blue velvet egg lined with golden starry paper. It was a dream. Never before had Susan seen anything so lovely... There was never one like it. She put it in her little drawer in the table where her treasures were kept, the book of pressed flowers, the book of texts in the shape of a bunch of violets, the velvet Christmas card with the silk fringe, and the card that came this Christmas.

Tenderly she touched them all. In the egg she placed her ring with the red stone, and a drop of quicksilver which had come from the barometer. She closed the drawer…

What a tale to tell the girls at school! She wouldn't take it there or it might get hurt, a rough boy might snatch it from her, or the teacher might see her with it and put it in her desk.

'Mother, may I ask someone to tea to see my egg?' she asked, fearing in her heart that no one would come so far.

'Yes, my dear,' and Margaret smiled at her enthusiasm, 'ask whoever you like…'

At break… Susan had a circle of girls round her… listening to the tale of the egg. They strolled under the chestnut trees with their arms round each other.

'It's blue velvet, sky-blue, and inside it is lined with paper covered with gold stars. It's the most beautiful egg I ever saw.' The girls opened their eyes and shook their curls in amazement.

'Bring it to school for us to see,' said Anne Frost, her friend.

'I daren't, Mother wouldn't let me, but you can come to tea and see it.'

'Can I?' asked one. 'Can I?' asked another.

Susan felt like a queen and invited them all. Big girls came to her, and she invited them. The rumour spread that Susan Garland was having a lot of girls to tea. Tiny little girls ran up and she said they might come too. She didn't know where to draw the line, and in the end the whole school of girls invited themselves…

Margaret happened to stand on the bank that day to watch for Susan's appearance at the end of the wood; she always felt slightly anxious if the child were late.

She could scarcely believe her eyes. There was Susan in her grey cape and the new scarlet tam-o'-shanter, but with her came a swarm of children. She had forgotten all about the vague invitation.

Was the child bringing the whole school home?

She ran back to the house and called Becky and Joshua. They stood dumbfounded, looking across the fields.

'We shall have to give them all something to eat, coming all that way,' she groaned.

'It will be like feeding the five thousand in the Bible,' exclaimed Becky, and Joshua stood gaping. He had never known such a thing. What had come over the little maid to ask such a rabble?

They went to the kitchen and dairy to take stock. There was Becky's new batch of bread, the great earthenware crock full to the brim, standing on the larder floor. There was a dish of butter ready for the shops, and baskets of eggs counted out, eighteen a shilling. There was a tin of brandy snaps, to last for months, some enormous jam pasties, besides three plum cakes.

They set to work, cutting and spreading on the big table, filling bread and butter plates with thick slices.

Joshua filled the copper kettles and put them on the fire, and counted out four dozen eggs, which he put on to boil. 'We can boil more when we've counted the lasses...'

'I've brought some girls to tea, Mother,' Susan said, opening her eyes at the preparations.

'Oh, indeed,' said Mrs Garland. 'How many have you brought?'

'A lot,' answered Susan. 'Where's my egg, they want to see it?'

'Susan Garland,' said Margaret severely, taking her by the shoulders, 'whatever do you mean by bringing all those girls home with you? Don't talk about that egg. Don't you see that they must all be fed? We can't let them come all this way without a good tea. You mustn't think of the egg, you will have to work.'

Susan looked aghast, she realized what she had done and began to cry.

'Never mind, dry your eyes at once and smile. I don't know what your father will say, but we will try to get them fed before he comes...'

Margaret gave out the cups and mugs herself, choosing clean, careful-looking girls for her best china...

Becky poured out the tea, and Susan took it to each girl, with new milk and brown sugar. Old Joshua, wearing an apron, walked along the rows with a clothes-basket of bread and butter and a basket of eggs. As soon as he got to the end he began again.

Margaret took over the tea, and sent Becky to cut more and more. Susan's legs ached and an immense hunger seized her, she had eaten nothing but sandwiches since her breakfast at half past seven. But there was no time, the girls clamoured for more, and she ran backwards and forwards with her four helpers, who had their own tea in between.

A clothes-basket was filled with cut-up pieces of cake, pastry, slabs of the men's cake, apple pasty, and currant slices. Then the box of ginger-snaps was taken round and some girls actually refused. The end was approaching, but still Joshua walked up and down the line with food...

At last the feast was finished and Becky and Margaret washed up the cups and mugs, and collected the egg-shells, whilst Joshua went milking and Susan ran for a ball to give them a game in the field before they went home. They ran races and played hide-and-seek, and lerky, they played tick-ticky-touch-stone round the great menhir, and swarmed over its surface.

At the end of an hour Margaret rang a bell and they came racing to her. 'Put on your coats now, my dears, and go home, your mothers will expect you, and you have a long walk before you.'

So they said goodbye, and ran off singing and happy, down the hill...

Susan went indoors and sat down, tired and famished, at the table. 'And, Mother, I never showed them my sky-blue egg after all! But they did enjoy themselves.'

The Best Easter Present Ever

SUE ATKINSON

It all started with Dad's Auntie Margaret. She disapproved of children having lots of chocolate eggs and bunnies at Easter and so, when Dad was a boy she used to arrive at his house and say 'I've brought you a funny-shaped Easter egg.' It would be a book, or a new jumper, or just the toy that he wanted.

Then, when my sister and I were little, she did the same for us. Each year Great-Aunt Margaret would arrive on Good Friday with her mysterious parcels and on Easter Day, before everyone else was up, Ali and I would go downstairs and rip off the paper before we started on the chocolate eggs from Mum and Dad and Gran.

The year I was nine, Great-Aunt Margaret gave me my own cricket bat; and then I was picked for the county under-eleven team for cricket. Dad was so proud of me. The bat is too small for me now but I keep it in a box in my wardrobe because it reminds me of those good times.

I miss Dad.

He went away before I got ill. I don't even know if he knows, because he never rings or writes letters. Mum doesn't even know where Dad is.

Why me? Why did I have to get sick? If it had been Ali she would have deserved it. I cried when I was in bed. I wanted to get well – but most of all I wanted Dad. Mum cried a lot too. I could hear her in her room at night.

No one knows how it happened; not even the doctors at the hospital. They said I might have caught a bug. All I know is that I kept feeling terrible and Mum kept telling me to go to bed early and Ali said I was a real wimp. I hit her. I knew Mum would shout at me but it was worth it.

Sometimes I really hate Ali. She makes me angry. She gets her friends round her – a load of giggly girls – and they walk across the bit of the playground at school where we are playing football and make silly faces at us. I want to smack her face but if I do, I'll get done; and our head teacher Mrs Wells is something else when she's mad. She always tells Mum too, so it's a no-win situation.

After a couple of weeks of this feeling dreadful, Mum took me to the doctor and he sent me straight to the hospital for tests. They said my kidneys weren't working and Mum cried and Ali laughed and shouted 'steak and kidney pie'. I was too ill to do anything but lie down. Worst of all, I was too ill to play in the area schools football league final. I had worked all season for that and then I couldn't play. We lost 5-4 and everyone said if I had been playing we would have won.

We had to go to the hospital three times a week. The hospital is miles from our house and my Mum can't afford a car so we had to get up at half-past six to get there by train. It was terrible. They put a needle in my arm and I had to lie in bed by this dialysis machine for hours. I was missing three days of school a week at first, and Mum had to change to working part-time, so we never had much money.

The thought of a second year of no football or cricket was terrible. From five years old, I had wanted to be a professional footballer or cricketer. Now I had to lie on the hospital bed for hours each week and I was too ill even to go into town on my own at weekends.

It was the worst time of my life. I couldn't stand the dialysis. It made me feel I was going to throw up. I missed three whole seasons of football. I had to eat special things. I wasn't allowed chocolate biscuits or crisps or peanuts and I had to take the most disgusting medicine you ever tasted. I had to get by on three drinks a day. Ali could have Coke when it was hot; I had to have just ice cubes.

I think I must have moaned a lot. On days I had to go to hospital, Ali went over the road to our neighbours, the Hunters. Ali got angry about this and argued with Mum: she wanted to stay on her own in the house. I couldn't see why Ali moaned so much because Mrs Hunter cooked her a big fry-up for breakfast – eggs, bacon, sausage: the lot – and when she went there after school she had cake and chocolate biscuits. Lucky thing. I can't eat things like that now.

Mum was always having to do special things for me, so I think Ali got jealous. She told me I was Mum's little precious, so I hit her again and she cut her eye and there was blood everywhere. Mum cried for hours that night and we all felt cross and I thought it was all my fault because I had bad kidneys.

I used to lie on the bed at night and in the renal unit at the hospital attached to that machine and think how great it would be if only Dad would come back.

Sometimes at weekends Mr Hunter pushed me on the cross-bar

of his bike up the park to see the football or cricket. A couple of times he persuaded Mum to let him take me to London to see a big match, but that made me tired and ill. Other times Mrs Wells drove the school minibus past our house and picked me up to watch a school match. She was really nice to me and said I was brave. She sometimes came round to bring books and to see how I was doing, keeping up with my school work.

The thought of year after year like this was awful. The doctor at the hospital said that what I really needed was a transplant and he would put my name on the list. He said I might feel much better if he could give me a new kidney and if the operation was a success. Mum wanted to give me one of her kidneys but when they tested her it wouldn't have worked. The new kidney had to be exactly the right kind. They found out that Ali's kitdney would be OK but Mum said no way. Ali kept saying she wanted to, but Mum just kept saying no.

The local paper found out about it and a lady came and took my picture and I was on the front page! 'Boy needs new kidney' it said. People sent me letters and cards and things. The vicar came round and brought me some comics. He showed me his donor card in his wallet and said he was putting donor cards in the church hall for people to pick up.

Then another journalist from the next town came to take my picture and they put it with other photos of other people in the area who needed new kidneys. I got loads more cards and letters and Mum stuck them up for me on my wall. Ali was furious because Mum has never let us stick things on the walls. She asked Mum if she could put up her Michael Jackson posters. Mum said no, and I made a face at Ali. Ali was really angry and when Mum had gone she said, 'One day I will get you, Rob.' After that we hardly spoke to each other. I tried to make out I didn't care.

Ali went out a lot with her friends. They went into town on the bus to go swimming and at the youth club they played table tennis and had barbecues in the summer. Sometimes she brought her friends home and they went into Ali's bedroom and played music loudly. I just kept out of the way.

At Easter I couldn't have any chocolate eggs of course, but Mrs West was taking some of us top class people to Windy Hill to roll our eggs. She said that when she was a little girl in Scotland, everyone did that. First we dyed them at school with onion skins and coloured inks and then we had egg rolling races. It was good fun.

But I was thirteen years old and I hardly had the strength to climb back up the hill after the first race. I had to sit down and watch the others. Ali was always calling me a wimp and I really felt like one.

That Easter, Great-Aunt Margaret didn't come to stay. But she sent us our funny-shaped Easter eggs. Mine was a really great space invader game that I could play while I was having dialysis at the hospital.

Then I changed to home dialysis. It didn't take nearly so long because of cutting out the travel to hospital. Mum was really nervous of it at first. You must keep things sterile – you know, really clean – and I think this drove her crazy. I felt so ill. I tried not to moan but from my bed I can see the park and I knew that my friends were out there playing football. I did manage to play sometimes, but I was so unfit that I had almost given up hope of ever playing sport seriously again.

Ali got a paper round. She was saving up for a denim jacket and a CD player. She used to count up her money on Saturday morning after she was paid and she kept it in her money box that Dad had given her when she was little.

Then one night it happened. The phone rang in the middle of the night and they told Mum to get me to hospital immediately. We were all rushing around saying 'don't panic'. Ali had come with us because Mum said she didn't have the nerve to ring the Hunters at two in the morning.

We got a taxi all the way to the hospital. It must have cost a fortune, but Ali said she would give Mum all her paper round money for the next six months to pay for it. That was the only time since I got ill that I thought that I would burst into tears in front of them both. Ali didn't look at me when she said it. She just stared out of the window, so I did the same.

The kidney was from a boy who had died in hospital. His parents came to see me while the nurse was getting me ready for the operation. I didn't know what to say to them. They don't normally let people meet like that but the boy's mum and dad said it helped them to see me. They nearly didn't let the doctors use the kidney, but they remembered seeing me in the paper and they wanted to help if they could. They were both crying.

I'm glad they did say yes.

I took ages to get over the operation, but that's a year ago now. I'm back in the county football team and next term I'm going to try for the county under fourteen cricket team.

I came home from hospital in an ambulance on Good Friday and loads of people were at our gate to cheer. I felt a bit stupid with them all standing there, but Mrs West had brought a huge chocolate egg from all my old teachers at middle school and Mr and Mrs Hunter gave Mum a huge bunch of daffodils from their garden. Ali and her friends had made a banner by painting an old sheet and it said 'Welcome home, Rob.' It had pictures of footballers all over it. They hung it with string out of the upstairs windows.

Great-Aunt Margaret had been at our house for a week, helping, so that Mum could get to the hospital to see me. There were two enormous parcels in the front room for Easter Day.

'Funny-shaped Easter eggs,' I said, feeling them all over.

'You have to wait until Easter Day,' said Great-Aunt Margaret, kissing me. As kissing aunts go, she really is one of the worst, but I knew Mum would tell me off if I wiped my face, so I just smiled at her. I was so happy to be home.

The grown-ups went into the kitchen for a cup of tea and Ali and I were left alone. I rubbed the kiss off hard with my sleeve.

'Glad you're home, Rob,' said Ali. 'I was really frightened that you might die.'

I didn't know what to say.

'Sorry I was so horrible to you,' she said.

'I was pretty terrible too,' I said. 'Friends now?'

'Yes,' said Ali and just for a moment she looked me straight in the face and she smiled at me.

On Easter Sunday morning I opened up my parcel. It was a really great pair of trainers, a new cricket ball, a track suit, and new football boots – just the right size. Mum had been in on all this. Ali had some trainers too, some jeans and a denim jacket.

'They are not all from me,' said Great-Aunt Margaret and she gave Mum a sideways look. There was a silence. I held my breath. I guessed some of them were from Dad, but I didn't dare say anything. Adults can be odd about that kind of thing.

Ali and I looked at each other. I knew we had both thought the same thing.

'I expect it's the best Easter present you've ever had,' said our aunt.

'Yes,' said Ali and I at the same time. We both started to giggle.

'Thank you,' I said looking at Ali. 'That really is the best Easter present I ever had.'

8
'It's All Right!'

Quarrels don't mend themselves. Someone has to put things right.
The Bible says that, instead of being God's friends,
'we were all like lost sheep, each one going its own way.'
But 'God loved the world so much' that he sent his own son, Jesus,
to put things right, though it cost him his life.
This section is about mending quarrels, righting wrongs, and
forgiving. *Stefan's Prisoner* is based on something that really happened.
And *Love Your Enemy* is a true story.

'Quarrel'

JEREMY CONSITT (AGED 11)

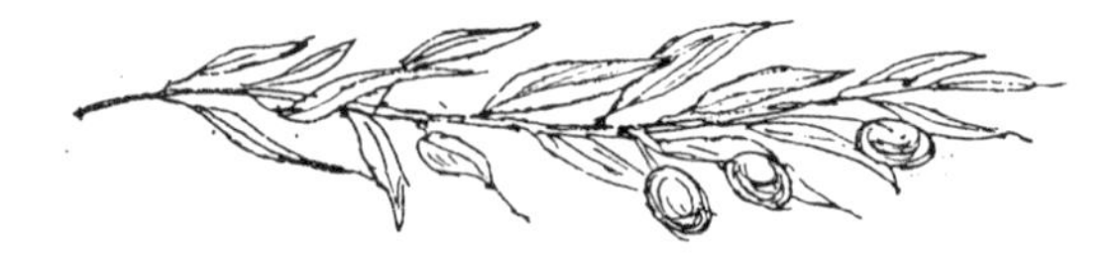

He didn't call for me on the way to school,
I played with somebody else.

I sat with someone else in assembly,
He looked upset but angry coming out.

I found a felt pen mark on my English book,
I put biro on his jumper.

I nudged him so his pencil slipped,
He nudged me and my pen slipped.

He fouled me in soccer,
I belted the ball at him.

He put yellow paint in my red,
I put yellow in his black.

I think he poked his tongue out at me,
I gently touched him.

He walked home with me as usual,
I called for him to see if he would play.

Elleni and the Sharing Bread

ARTHUR SCHOLEY

The story goes that once upon a time, at the foot of a great mountain, there were two villages, one on each side of the river. The people of each village hated the other with a great hatred. No boats crossed the water that rushed between them. And if the other village was mentioned at all, it was with a curse.

Elleni, youngest daughter of the village chief Allarik, could not understand why.

'How did the hatred begin?' she asked.

'More questions!' said her father. 'It has always been so, and it will always be so.'

And her mother said: 'Be grateful that you live in *this* village, Elleni.'

She asked her older sisters and brothers as she helped to bring in the wheat in the fields under the mountain.

'Oh it was a quarrel,' said one. 'Two brothers quarrelled, so I heard. One took his family to live across the other side. Long time ago now.'

'They stole grain in the night!' said another. 'That's how it started. Of course, we do have the best wheat fields this side.'

'Oh, they are a bad lot, the other villagers, Elleni. They do strange and wicked things. Forget about them.'

It was that year that great fear came down from the Mountain, brought by Brendik, the youngest of the shepherds. He ran through the fields, shouting to the villagers who were now bringing in the last of the wheat. He staggered into the village. Straight to the Hall of Meetings he went and hammered loudly on the summoning bell. As soon as Allarik and the others began to crowd in, he blurted out:

'There is danger. You must move out of the village!'

'What do you mean? What's happened?' Allarik demanded.

'In the night,' said the young shepherd, 'there was a terrible noise like thunder. Stones, boulders, came rushing down the mountainside and blocked the river that flows into our river. A deep lake is building up, crashing against the rocks. Soon it will all come bursting down. We must move out, now. The water is pushing all along the stones. Look. It could break through the east side of the ridge and come straight down on us. Or...'

'Well, go on,' cried the villagers.

'Or if it breaks through the western ridge, well, it will fall on the other village.'

A grim smile came for a moment on Allarik's face. Then he turned to the villagers.

'Come, everyone! There is no time to lose. Pack your belongings – everything you value. We must climb to the South Hill. We'll camp there until the mountain decides between us.'

In the turmoil, Elleni had a question for her father:

'But shouldn't we send a message to the other village, to warn them too?'

'Are you mad, girl?' Allarik shouted. 'Let them see to themselves. Help your mother and sister pack the food!' He laughed angrily. 'Warn the other village? What next!'

That night on the South Hill the campfire flickered on stern faces as the villagers sat still, praying and listening. As the sun rose their eyes searched the area beneath the mountain. Now they could see the high wall of boulders. Their eyes grew wide with fear at the thought of the water building up behind it.

For three days they waited. Then, on the third day, just after dawn, it came. With a crashing roar the torrent of rock and flood burst open and down towards the ridge before them.

At first the ridge held firm. Then, as the water and rock continued to pound, it began to shift. It was going to give – but which side would give, which side? In a few seconds they knew. Let there be praise! It was the west side, the part furthest away from them, that began to crumble. With a deafening roar, the torrent burst through in its next angry rush – straight down to the other village.

Laughing and singing, the villagers on South Hill gathered their belongings, dismantled their makeshift shelters, stamped out the fires and ran to their safe homes. As they passed the Hall of Meetings, Allarik called out, 'Finish bringing in the wheat. Return here this afternoon. We'll have the Sharing Bread, and we'll sacrifice to the Mountain. Then we'll have our harvest feast!'

At home, Elleni's mother bustled into the kitchen.

'Elleni, girl, I've not heard that corn-stone grind these last ten minutes. Don't sit gazing ahead, doing nothing.'

'Mother,' Elleni asked, 'those people in the other village. What has happened to them?'

Her mother stopped for a moment and sighed. Yes, she thought, what has happened to them? Then she turned angrily.

'Think what will happen to you, girl, if that flour is not ready. It's your turn to bring the corn for the Sharing Bread. It's your turn to present the bread in the Place of Meetings this afternoon. Will you bring disgrace on your father's house?'

Elleni pulled the great stone round, crushing the grains of wheat. The first of the flour trickled through onto the ground.

The Place of Meetings was full. No one could remember the tables being piled so high with food. There would be so much to enjoy: eating, drinking, dancing far into the night.

Now Allarik called for silence.

'Let us give praise and thanks for our safety and for our harvest,' he said. 'The mountain has saved us and our village, and...' he paused. In his mind again, and into the minds of all the villagers, now that the busy preparations were done, came thoughts of the other village. Allarik shook himself, and spoke again. 'The Sharing Bread,' he said abruptly, turning to Elleni. She brought forward the large flat, round loaf.

Allarik reminded them: 'Each family will break off a piece, and each member will share it. But take one piece back with you tonight to place beneath your hearth stone, so that good fortune will be with you throughout the coming year.'

Again he stopped. All had heard the noise. Someone was outside. There was a scuttling of stones, a dragging of feet, and a heavy groaning. Then into the open doorway stepped a terrible figure – a man, exhausted, wild-eyed. His rags clung wetly to his bruised body. He staggered against the doorpost and would have fallen. But he took hold of himself and came up to Allarik.

'Please help us. We have nothing, nothing. Our houses are gone. Many are dead, others trapped in the ruins, children screaming for their parents. Even the living will soon die if we don't get food – and you have' – his eyes gazed at the tables – 'you have all this.'

The villagers had pushed back against the walls, staring. He was from the other village!

'I swam across the river,' he said. 'You must help us.' He held out his hand and slowly turned around, looking pleadingly at them all. No one spoke or moved.

In the silence, he turned back to Allarik, disbelief in his eyes. Was no one going to help? Then it was that Elleni, still holding the Sharing Bread, went up to him. She broke off a piece of bread, and put it into his hand.

A sigh of agreement went through the Place of Meetings. Allarik stepped forward and put his arm round Elleni.

'Oh, my people, we are in great shame for the terrible things we have done. It has taken a child to show us what we buried in our hearts.' He grasped the other villager's hand which still had in it the piece of Sharing Bread. 'We have done you great wrong,' he said. 'Forgive us all.' He turned to the villagers.

'There will be no feast until the other village is fed.' He held up the Bread. 'Let none share this who does not also share this promise.'

Taking the food from the tables, the villagers sped to their houses for more. They rushed down to the river bank, and into their boats, to cross over to the other village...

'Hands'

CLARE BROOKS (AGED 6)

Stealing, killing
Wicked hands
Wretched, terrible
Cruel hands.
Slapping, punching
Naughty hands.
Bad hands,
Bad hands.

Praying, helping,
Kind hands.
Clapping, shaking,
Friendly hands.
Patting, giving,
Loving hands.
Good hands,
Good hands.

Stefan's Prisoner

From *Dark Journey*

JENNY ROBERTSON

Stefan's country has become a police state, where it is dangerous to talk about God or go to church. In trouble for tearing down a Party banner, he is sentenced to hard labour. In the camp, Nik (Brother Nikolai), steps in to save Stefan in a way he can never forget.

Stefan is set free, only to be called up for Army service. Major Grania orders Stefan and Gruzek to rough up the political prisoners. Which is how Prisoner XR7 gets his hands so badly broken. Now Stefan is alone with the prisoner...

'You can't work against this system,' Nik had said. 'It will break you.'

But prisoner XR7 hadn't been broken. He stood gazing out of the barred window, and Stefan blew no smoke in his direction.

The guard brought in Stefan's breakfast: soft rolls, eggs, sour milk, coffee. XR7 was given no food, only hot water. His broken fingers could scarcely lift the mug he rested on his knee.

'Why don't they give you food, XR7?' asked Stefan.

'In the punishment cells we do not eat every day, Comrade Supervisor.'

'Aren't you hungry?'

'One gets used to hunger.'

But it seemed to Stefan that the prisoner looked longingly at the fresh white bread.

'I didn't!' The words burst out of Stefan and he glanced at once towards the peep-hole.

Were they observed? It was hard to say.

'How old are you?' Stefan asked suddenly.

The prisoner hesitated. 'Why do you ask me that, sir?'

Odd how the old-fashioned title 'sir' seemed so right from his lips. But he shouldn't be calling me that, thought Stefan. And he's right. I'm not here to ask personal questions.

Aloud he said, 'You remind me of someone I knew. He's dead now. I kind of have the feeling you're not as old as you look.'

The prisoner smiled at that.

'Someone as young as you, Comrade Supervisor, will think I'm very old, but in fact I'm not yet forty.'

Stefan glanced back at the peep-hole.

'Let the enemies of our people perish,' he announced to any listening ear.

He still had one roll left to eat, but he didn't feel hungry now. Still, why waste good bread? He slipped his roll into the wallet Marylla had given him, then he unlocked the cell door and strolled casually along the corridor for his shower, taking his time under the warm water.

Anything rather than return to bait this man! Memories of Nik made it harder than ever to carry out his orders. 'Oh God, help me,' he prayed as he went back to the cell.

XR7 was standing beside the window, singing softly.

'Will it disturb you if I stay here for a little, sir?'

'Stand there if you like... though there's nothing much to see.'

'Just the morning sun shining on the wall opposite.' He tried to point but his trousers slipped again.

'You need a belt, or a bootlace, or a bit of string, but of course they're not allowed here.' Stefan recalled his lectures. 'Safety first,' Grania had explained. 'Prisoners might do themselves in.' Not this man, though, thought Stefan and aloud he asked, 'Aren't you allowed warm clothes either?'

'The cold is harder to bear than hunger. But spring has touched the world beyond these walls. It's Easter Day.'

'They call it Easter Chick time now,' Stefan reminded him. His thoughts flashed back to the Young Progress Camp with Marylla. Could it really be a whole year ago? Perhaps Marylla would be back at the camp, one of the leaders this time. His mother would be standing outside the locked church in Lipa singing Easter hymns with other village women. In the Easters of his childhood bells echoed over the fields. Children took painted eggs to church in little baskets. Gran always made sure his basket was lined with a cloth she had embroidered herself. It came out every Easter, bleached and starched and pressed. 'Christ has risen from the dead,' she would say, and the bells and Easter hymns took up the words.

Now, in a cold punishment cell, Stefan heard a prisoner sing the old Easter hymns. And he panicked.

'Shut up! Do you hear me? Shut up!' He pulled the prisoner back from the window. 'You'll get me into trouble with all your hymns.'

XR7 turned from Stefan and started to pace up and down the cell.

'What's the matter? Aren't you well?'

'I'm well enough, Comrade Supervisor.'

His deference riled Stefan. 'What are you in for? Saying prayers?'

For answer the prisoner pointed to the label on his shirt.

'Ex-pers. Anti-regime activity.'

Ex-pers? Like Nik.

'A life sentence?' Stefan asked.

He nodded.

The guard took away Stefan's dirty plates. If I don't hurry up and attack him they'll take me away too, he thought. But he had no heart for this assignment. Why the hell had Gruzek gone? He lit another cigarette and stood looking out of the window.

Beside him XR7 knelt to pray.

And what was Stefan supposed to do? Beat him to a pulp?

Prayer isn't forbidden, he told an imaginary Grania. Anyway, his thoughts went on, what right has the regime to take our Easter celebrations from us?

XR7 seemed oblivious of his surroundings now. He prayed quietly, but Stefan caught the words, 'I hold before you broken hands instead of bread.'

Now Stefan understood why the unfed prisoner had looked longingly at his bread.

Yet in his wallet he still had a fresh white roll. Even a crumb would be enough to let the prisoner celebrate his Easter feast.

Stefan held out his bread.

'What is it, sir?' the prisoner whispered.

'Take it. Be quick.'

The prisoner pressed swollen lips against Stefan's hand. 'Thank you, oh, thank you.'

Broken hands held broken bread.

Gran, Mother, Sister Helen – they all believed like this. Words from Stefan's childhood, half remembered, improperly understood.

'This is my body, broken for you... my blood, shed for your forgiveness.'

Broken. Yes, he knew all about being broken. But forgiveness? No, not for Stefan, whose assignment was murder.

But now the prisoner was on his feet, smiling at him.

'I can never thank you enough.'

And Stefan didn't know what to reply.

'My mother believes like you,' he blurted out, perhaps because the man's Easter hymns had stirred thoughts of his home and family. 'And there's someone else in our village. Sister Helen. She used to teach us prayers, but they made her stop.' He broke off and burst out with the thing uppermost in his mind. 'Did you know they put us in here to kill you?'

'I guessed as much. And after me there will be others. They want to brutalize you.'

'They reckon we're brutes already. We'd all had prison sentences. But don't worry. I can't kill you now. I doubt if I ever would have been able to.' He sat down on his mattress. 'Gruzek's lucky. He's well out of this. What went wrong, I wonder? Who moved him?' He looked helplessly at the prisoner, and the man's broken hands made a gesture towards him.

'Don't despair,' he said. 'I have seen love and mercy work in the most hopeless places.'

'Live!'

EMILY DICKINSON

Love is the fellow
of the resurrection,
scooping up the dust
and chanting, 'Live!'

Paradise Hill

From *The Little White Horse*

ELIZABETH GOUDGE

When Maria Merryweather comes to Moonacre Manor she finds a great many things that need to be put right. Loveday Minette and Sir Benjamin have never made up their ridiculous quarrel over the pink geraniums. More serious still is the centuries-old quarrel that began with the unhappy Moon Princess and her dowry of pearls. Maria, with the help of her very special friend Robin, is determined to restore peace and happiness to the whole of Moonacre valley. She begins with the land which her own ancestor, Sir Wrolf, took from the monks long ago: Paradise Hill must be given back to God...

The church was full of sunshine, children, and music. Old Parson was standing at the chancel steps with his fiddle tucked under his chin, playing one of the loveliest tunes that Maria had ever heard, and sitting all round him on the steps were all the children of Silverydew, in their bright clothes like flowers, singing as the birds sing in the dawn, with all their power and joy.

Old Parson did not stop playing as Loveday Minette, Maria, Wrolf, Periwinkle, Zachariah, Serena, and Wiggins* joined the group of singing children, but he called out to them: 'Take your places and pick up the words and the tune of this new song as quickly as you can.'

Loveday and Maria sat down on the steps with Wiggins and Serena on their laps, and Wrolf and Periwinkle standing patiently and reverently beside them, and set themselves to the learning of this new song... But Zachariah leaped over the top of the door that led into the Merryweather pew, and sat himself down inside upon the cushions as though he were all the Pharaohs who had ever lived combined into one magnificent purring personage.

* Wrolf is the Merryweathers' lion-like dog and Periwinkle is Maria's pony. Then there is Zachariah, the cat; Serena, the hare; and Wiggins – Maria's beautiful but very spoiled little dog.

The words of the new song that Old Parson had written for this historic occasion were easy to pick up, and Loveday and Maria were soon singing them as lustily as any child present.

Spring Song

Praised be our Lord for our brother the sun,
Most comely is he, and bright.
Praised be our Lord for our sister the moon,
With her pure and lovely light.
Praised be our Lord for the sparkling bright stars
Encircling the dome of night.

Praised be our Lord for the wind and the rain,
For clouds, for dew and the air;
For the rainbow set in the sky above
Most precious and kind and fair.
For all these things tell the love of our Lord,
The love that is everywhere.

Praised be our Lord for our mother the earth,
Most gracious is she, and good,
With her gifts of flowers and nuts and fruit,
Of grass and corn and wood,
For she it is who upholds us in life
And gives us our daily food.

Praised be our Lord for the turn of the year,
For new-born life upspringing;
For buds and for blossoms, for lambs and babes,
For thrush and blackbird singing.
May praise, like the lark, leap up from our hearts,
To Heaven's gate upwinging.

'That will do, I think,' said Old Parson, when everyone was singing to his satisfaction. 'Maria, will you please go to the Merryweather Chantry, and see whether Robin has finished the task that I set him there.'

Maria put down Serena, who was in her lap, and hurried to the chantry. Robin was seated cross-legged on the floor, his back against

Sir Wrolf's tomb. Sir Wrolf's great cross-handled sword was laid across his knees and he was scrubbing it vigorously with emery paper. When he saw Maria he looked up and grinned. 'I can't make the steel come really clean and bright,' he said, 'it's too old. But it's better than it was. We're to take it with us, Old Parson says.'

Maria dimpled with pleasure. That was a good idea of Old Parson's! Sir Wrolf himself couldn't come with them to restore the property that he had stolen, but at least they could take his sword!

Robin got up and dusted himself, put the emery paper neatly away with his scrubbing-brush and pail in the corner of the chantry, and he and Maria together carried the sword to Old Parson. When they got back to the chancel steps again Old Parson had put away his violin and hitched up his cassocks, and Loveday Minette was lifting the statue of the Lady and the Child down from its niche, and the children were taking the Bell from its place by the pulpit.

'Are we taking them?' asked Maria.

'Of course,' said Old Parson, 'they are monastery property, and we are going to restore them to where they belong.'

Some of the children were a bit tearful. 'We shall miss the Lady dreadfully,' they lamented.

'Nonsense,' said Old Parson. 'You can take your gifts to her on Paradise Hill just as well as here. From this day on we shall be going there often to praise God. Now come along, all of you. We are going there in procession this very moment. I will go first and the rest of you, animals and children, will follow me two by two, singing that song of praise that I have just taught you, at the tops of your voices.

You can take it in turns to carry the Lady and the Bell.'

'We shall look like the animals going into the ark,' said Maria.

'We could not look like anything better,' said Old Parson. 'Come along now. Robin, give me the sword.'

Robin gave him the great cross-handled sword and, holding it aloft like a processional cross, Old Parson went striding down the aisle with it and out into the sunshine, singing at the top of his voice. And close behind him, side by side, went Wrolf and Periwinkle, and behind them went Maria and Robin, with Wiggins and Zachariah making a pair behind them, and then came Loveday Minette... followed by... all the other children, carrying the Lady and the Bell, lustily singing the song Old Parson had taught them.

By the time they reached the steep lane the sun was high in the sky and it was the most glorious spring morning ever seen. As they climbed upwards, still singing, though rather breathlessly now, the children picked the ferns and periwinkles and primroses and made them into great bunches. And all about them the birds were singing too, carolling so loudly that the noise they made nearly drowned the children's singing. When they came out from the lane on to Paradise Hill the sun seemed to blaze more gloriously than ever, and, climbing the hill, they all felt very happy, making their way in and out between the sheep and the frisking lambs, over the bright green grass and purple violets, past the blossoming thorn-tree, up and up to where the beech-trees reared their silver and green against the blue sky. When they were nearly at the summit Old Parson made them stop and get their breath back, and then, singing once again, they made their way beneath the branches of the beech-trees and through the doorway in the broken wall and into the paved court beyond...

[Old Parson] must have laboured half the night, for [inside] the paving-stones had been cleared of all the rubbish, the weeds and brambles, and had been washed and scrubbed so that they reflected the sun's light like slabs of pearl. And the well and the channel through the paving-stones had been cleared of dead leaves, so that the spring bubbled up clear and strong and then ran away quickly and easily, as bright as silver, through the low archway beneath the rowan-tree. The tree looked glorious in the morning sunlight, its berries bright as lighted candles, and beneath its branches Old Parson had piled up the stones that he had cleared from the court into a little altar. The whole place looked fresh and clean and lovely, and utterly made new, and when Old Parson had thrust Sir Wrolf's sword into the branches of the rowan-tree, so that it stood behind the stone altar like a cross, with the children's flowers piled before it, and the statue of the Lady and her Child had been set in the empty niche above the low stone archway, and the Bell had been hung from a branch of the old holly, the whole place was ready for the prayers and praises which Old Parson proceeded to offer there.

First, standing before the altar with Loveday, the children and the animals grouped about him, with as many of the sheep and lambs as had been able to squeeze their way into the already overcrowded little court, he said a very long prayer, though as it was such a lovely morning nobody minded. He prayed for forgiveness for Sir Wrolf, who had stolen this place from God – and at this point the living Wrolf gave a deep penitent growl. And then he prayed for forgiveness for all the Merryweathers who during succeeding generations had neglected to give it back – and here Loveday Minette and Maria and Robin bowed their heads and said they were sorry. And then he prayed for further forgiveness for the Merryweathers because they kept for themselves the money they had got from selling the wool off the backs of the sheep who were pastured on this holy hill – and at this point all the sheep baaed distressfully. And then he prayed that for ever and ever this place should now be a holy place, and that no wickedness should be done here any more. And then they all said Amen, and the sheep baaed low and mysteriously, and Robin went to the holly-tree and set the Bell swinging, and its deep voice sounded out loud and clear to tell the people in the valley below that once more Paradise Hill belonged to God. And then Robin took his shepherd's pipe... and to its accompaniment they sang 'The Lord is my Shepherd' and 'The Old Hundredth', and the Bell Song and the Spring Song, and all the praising things they could think of. And then at last, reluctantly, because it was so lovely up here on the hill, they turned themselves about and went in procession back to the village, singing all the way.

And when they got to the village they found that the sound of the Bell, and of the joyous singing, had brought all the grown-ups out into the village street, and they were laughing and talking and crying all together because they were so happy. For the spring had come and Paradise Hill had been given back to God, and they felt they were all in a fair way now to live happy ever after.

'Real Forgiveness'

CORAL RUMBLE

For the very first time
I understand
What real forgiveness is;
But my brother needs it
More than me,
The fault is always his!

Love Your Enemy

From *Tramp for the Lord*

CORRIE TEN BOOM

Corrie and Betsie, two sisters from Holland, were taken to Ravensbruck concentration camp during the Second World War, for helping Jews to escape from the Nazis. They were brutally treated, and Betsie died. Now, two years after the end of the war, Corrie has come to a church in Germany to speak about forgiving...

'When we confess our sins,' I said, 'God casts them into the deepest ocean, gone forever. And even though I cannot find a Scripture for it, I believe God then places a sign out there that says, NO FISHING ALLOWED.'

The solemn faces stared back at me, not quite daring to believe. There were never questions after a talk in Germany in 1947. People stood up in silence, in silence collected their wraps, in silence left the room.

And that's when I saw him, working his way forward against the others. One moment I saw the overcoat and the brown hat; the next, a blue uniform and a visored cap with its skull and crossbones. It came back with a rush; the huge room with its harsh overhead lights; the pathetic pile of dresses and shoes in the centre of the floor; the shame of walking naked past this man. I could see my sister's frail form ahead of me, ribs sharp beneath the parchment skin. *Betsie, how thin you were!*

The place was Ravensbruck and the man who was making his way forward had been a guard – one of the most cruel guards.

Now he was in front of me, hand thrust out: 'A fine message, Fräulein! How good it is to know that, as you say, all our sins are at the bottom of the sea!'

And I, who had spoken so glibly of forgiveness, fumbled in my pocketbook rather than take that hand. He would not remember me, of course – how could he remember one prisoner among those thousands of women?

But I remembered him and the leather crop swinging from his belt. I was face-to-face with one of my captors and my blood seemed to freeze.

'You mentioned Ravensbruck in your talk,' he was saying. 'I was a guard there.' No, he did not remember me.

'But since that time,' he went on, 'I have become a Christian. I know that God has forgiven me for the cruel things I did there, but I would like to hear it from your lips as well. Fräulein,' – again the hand came out – 'will you forgive me?'

And I stood there – I whose sins had again and again to be forgiven – and could not forgive. Betsie had died in that place – could he erase her slow terrible death simply for the asking?

It could not have been many seconds that he stood there – hand held out – but to me it seemed hours as I wrestled with the most difficult thing I had ever had to do.

For I had to do it – I knew that. The message that God forgives has a prior condition: that we forgive those who have injured us. 'If you do not forgive men their trespasses,' Jesus says, 'neither will your Father in heaven forgive your trespasses.'

I knew it not only as a commandment of God, but as a daily experience. Since the end of the war I had had a home in Holland for victims of Nazi brutality. Those who were able to forgive their former enemies were able also to return to the outside world and rebuild their lives, no matter what the physical scars. Those who nursed their bitterness remained invalids. It was as simple and as horrible as that.

And still I stood there with the coldness clutching my heart. But forgiveness is not an emotion – I knew that too. Forgiveness is an act of the will, and the will can function regardless of the temperature of the heart. 'Jesus, help me!' I prayed silently. 'I can lift my hand. I can do that much. You supply the feeling.'

And so woodenly, mechanically, I thrust my hand into the one stretched out to me. And as I did, an incredible thing took place. The current started in my shoulder, raced down my arm, sprang into our joined hands. And then this healing warmth seemed to flood my whole being, bringing tears to my eyes.

'I forgive you, brother!' I cried. 'With all my heart.'

9
A New Beginning

Easter, for Christians, means a new beginning. Jesus died, but he won the fight against death. He is alive – for ever. And he shares this new life with everyone who follows him. A new life, here and now. A life that not even death can end!

So the poems and stories in this last section are all about new life. In *The Oak Tree* it's the death of the oak that allows the new seedlings to grow. In the extract from *Charlotte's Web*, Wilbur the pig has to lose his best friend to find joy on the other side of sadness. And in the last two stories, a goose called Gloria and Geronimo Grub both find a new life that is wonderful beyond imagining.

'Love is Come Again'

J.M. CRUM

Now the green blade riseth from the buried grain,
Wheat that in dark earth many days has lain;
Love lives again, that with the dead has been;
Love is come again,
Like wheat that springeth green.

In the grave they laid him, Love whom men had slain,
Thinking that never he would wake again,
Laid in the earth like grain that sleeps unseen:
Love is come again,
Like wheat that springeth green...

When our hearts are wintry, grieving, or in pain,
Thy touch can call us back to life again,
Fields of our hearts that dead and bare have been;
Love is come again,
Like wheat that springeth green.

The Oak Tree

FAY SAMPSON

There was a roar of thunder. It made Darren and Linda jump. The lights flickered and went out for a moment. Paddy, their black mongrel dog, whimpered and crawled under the sofa.

'That was a bit close,' said Mum.

Dad pulled out the plug from the television set.

'Better be on the safe side,' he said.

'Why did you do that?' complained Darren. 'I was watching the film.'

'This storm's almost overhead. The chances are tens of thousands to one against it hitting us. But if lightning did strike the television aerial it could run down the wires and do a bit of damage.'

'Could it really hit our house?' asked Linda.

She got down on her knees to cuddle Paddy. The room didn't seem quite as safe as before.

'It's not very likely,' comforted Dad. 'Lightning usually strikes the highest thing. And there are trees around us taller than our chimney.'

With the television turned off, the storm seemed louder than ever. They could see the lightning flashing through the curtains. There was a tearing noise as the electricity streaked towards the earth, and then a tremendous bang of thunder. It was hard not to feel frightened.

'It's not right over us,' said Mum. 'Count the time between the lightning and the thunder. It's supposed to be a mile for every five seconds.'

But at the same time there was a brilliant flash and an explosion so loud it made them all cry out. Paddy burst out barking. The house shook and all the lights went dark. This time they stayed out. But outside there was a leaping blue light. They smelt burning.

'Stay there,' cried Dad, rushing to the front door. But nobody did.

They all ran into the garden. Darren whirled round, expecting to see the roof on fire. But no, their house was dark and safe.

Something else had caught that stroke of lightning. The huge oak tree at the end of the garden was ablaze. The bare winter twigs were blossoming with sparks. Boughs roared and crackled. Fiery branches broke off and plunged to the ground. Flames were even running down its mighty trunk.

After the first horrified cry, no one could speak. The great tree was dying before their eyes.

Then torrents of rain came pelting down. The flames of the burning oak began to hiss and die down.

'Indoors,' ordered Mum. 'There's nothing we can do.'

Inside the house, the lights came on again.

'Will it strike *us* now?' asked Linda, stroking the trembling Paddy.

'Listen,' said Dad, as the lightning flared again.

The children counted slowly to twenty-five. Then the thunder rumbled.

'It's all right,' said Darren. 'It's going away.'

Linda rubbed her eyes. The bedroom was full of light. She must have overslept. She ran to the window and pulled back the curtains.

What she saw made her gasp. The morning sun had always reached her room through a pattern of branches or a screen of leaves. But the boughs had gone. The oak tree was dead.

It was a terrible sight. Black, splintered limbs pointed at the winter sky. The great trunk was split.

'Darren!' she called. 'Come and look at the oak tree!'

He came from his bedroom into hers. They stared out in silence.

Darren said what they were both thinking.

'If it hadn't been for that tree, the lightning might have struck us.'

Spring came, and the green spears of bulbs began to push up through the brown earth of the garden.

Darren, Linda and Mum were taking Paddy for a run in the field behind the house. As they panted back to the hedge at the bottom of the garden, Darren stopped.

'What are these funny little plants? I don't remember seeing them before.'

Mum caught them up.

'Don't you recognize them? Those curling edges on the leaves?'

Linda bent down, frowning.

'I've seen leaves this shape somewhere. I know! They're like the oak tree's!'

Mum burst out laughing.

'Of course they are! These *are* oaks.'

'Baby oaks?' cried Darren. 'You mean, these will grow into great trees, like the one the lightning struck?'

'Then why haven't we found them before?' asked Linda. 'They never used to grow in the grass.'

'Because our oak tree died,' said Mum, looking up at the leafless skeleton. 'For hundreds of years it stood there. A full grown tree can drink a hundred gallons of water every day. Its leaves keep the sunlight from reaching the ground beneath. It had to die before the baby trees could live.'

'But how did they get there?' wondered Darren.

'From seeds.'

'Seeds! You can't go into a garden shop and ask for oak seeds!'

'I bet I know!' Linda's fingers were digging into the soil. Paddy tried to help.

Carefully she uncovered a root. The once-glossy nut had shrivelled and split. A woody stem was springing from it. At its tip, a cluster of leaves was unfurling in the sunshine.

'Of course!' cried Darren. 'An acorn!'

He picked up a handful of earth. 'It's so crumbly and dark.'

Mum said, 'All these centuries the oak tree has been dropping its leaves here, and their goodness has rotted back into the soil. It may have died. But now it has given life too.'

They came back into the garden. Linda turned and laid her hand against the old oak's trunk.

'Thank you,' she whispered. 'We'll always remember you.'

‘The Easter Worm’

CORAL RUMBLE

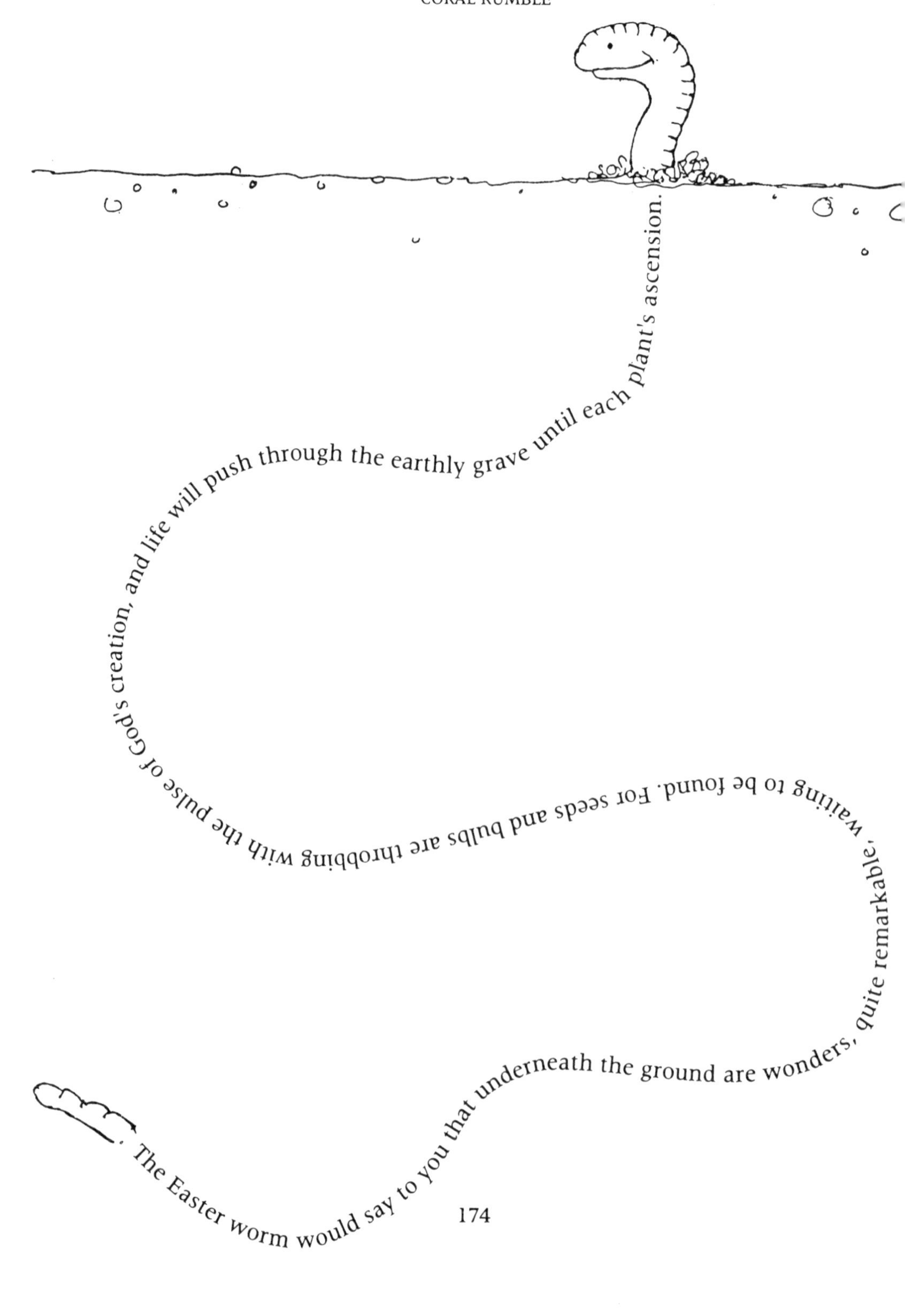

Charlotte's Last Day

From *Charlotte's Web*

E.B. WHITE

Charlotte the spider and Wilbur the pig are friends. Thanks to Charlotte's cleverness, Wilbur has become a Prize Pig. The Zuckermans will never let him leave the farm now. She has saved his bacon! Everything should be wonderful but, while Templeton the rat sleeps peacefully, Charlotte, exhausted by producing her egg sac of babies, tells Wilbur some terrible news...

Charlotte and Wilbur were alone... Templeton was asleep. Wilbur lay resting after the excitement and strain of the ceremony. His medal still hung from his neck; by looking out of the corner of his eye he could see it.

'Charlotte,' said Wilbur after a while, 'why are you so quiet?'

'I like to sit still,' she said. 'I've always been rather quiet.'

'Yes, but you seem specially so today. Do you feel all right?'

'A little tired, perhaps. But I feel peaceful. Your success in the ring this morning was, to a small degree, *my* success. Your future is assured. You will live, secure and safe, Wilbur. Nothing can harm you now. These autumn days will shorten and grow cold. The leaves will shake loose from the trees and fall. Christmas will come, then the snows of winter. You will live to enjoy the beauty of the frozen world, for you mean a great deal to Zuckerman and he will not harm you, ever. Winter will pass, the days will lengthen, the ice will melt in the pasture pond. The song sparrow will return and sing, the frogs will awake, the warm wind will blow again. All these sights and sounds and smells will be yours to enjoy Wilbur – this lovely world, these golden days...'

Charlotte stopped. A moment later a tear came to Wilbur's eye. 'Oh, Charlotte,' he said. 'To think that when I first met you I thought you were cruel and bloodthirsty!'

When he recovered from his emotion, he spoke again.

'Why did you do all this for me?' he asked. 'I don't deserve it. I've never done anything for you.'

'You have been my friend,' replied Charlotte. 'That in itself is a tremendous.thing. I wove my webs for you because I liked you. After all, what's a life, anyway? We're born, we live a little while, we die. A spider's life can't help being something of a mess, with all this trapping and eating flies. By helping you, perhaps I was trying to lift up my life a trifle. Heaven knows anyone's life can stand a little of that.'

'Well,' said Wilbur, 'I'm no good at making speeches. I haven't got your gift for words. But you have saved me, Charlotte, and I would gladly give my life for you – I really would.'

'I'm sure you would. And I thank you for your generous sentiments.'

'Charlotte,' said Wilbur. 'We're all going home today. The Fair is almost over. Won't it be wonderful to be back home in the barn cellar again with the sheep and the geese? Aren't you anxious to get home?'

For a moment Charlotte said nothing. Then she spoke in a voice so low Wilbur could hardly hear the words.

'I will not be going back to the barn,' she said.

Wilbur leapt to his feet. 'Not going back?' he cried. 'Charlotte, what are you talking about?'

'I'm done for,' she replied. 'In a day or two I'll be dead. I haven't even strength enough to climb down into the crate. I doubt if I have enough silk in my spinneret to lower me to the ground.'

Hearing this, Wilbur threw himself down in an agony of pain and sorrow. Great sobs racked his body. He heaved and grunted with desolation. 'Charlotte,' he moaned. 'Charlotte! My true friend!'

'Come now, let's not make a scene,' said the spider. 'Be quiet, Wilbur. Stop thrashing about!'

'But I can't *stand* it,' shouted Wilbur. 'I won't leave you here alone to die. If you're going to stay here I shall stay, too.'

'Don't be ridiculous,' said Charlotte... 'The others will be back any minute now, and they'll shove you into that crate and away you'll go. Besides, it wouldn't make any sense for you to stay. There would be no one to feed you. The Fair Grounds will soon be empty and deserted.'

Wilbur was in a panic. He raced round and round the pen. Suddenly he had an idea – he thought of the egg sac and the five hundred and fourteen little spiders that would hatch in the spring. If Charlotte herself was unable to go home to the barn, at least he must take her children along.

Wilbur rushed to the front of his pen. He put his front feet up on the top board and gazed around. In the distance he saw… the Zuckermans approaching. He knew he would have to act quickly.

'Where's Templeton?' he demanded.

'He's in the corner, under the straw, asleep,' said Charlotte.

Wilbur rushed over, pushed his strong snout under the rat, and tossed him into the air.

'Templeton!' screamed Wilbur. 'Pay attention!'

The rat, surprised out of a sound sleep, looked first dazed then disgusted.

'What kind of monkeyshine is this?' he growled. 'Can't a rat catch a wink of sleep without being rudely popped into the air?'

'Listen to me!' cried Wilbur. 'Charlotte is very ill. She has only a short time to live. She cannot accompany us home, because of her condition. Therefore, it is absolutely necessary that I take her egg sac with me. I can't reach it, and I can't climb. You are the only one that can get it. There's not a second to be lost. The people are coming – they'll be here in no time. Please, please, *please*, Templeton, climb up and get the egg sac.'

The rat yawned. He straightened his whiskers. Then he looked up at the egg sac.

'So!' he said in disgust. 'So it's old Templeton to the rescue again, is it? Templeton do this, Templeton do that, Templeton please run down to the dump and get me a magazine clipping, Templeton please lend me a piece of string so I can spin a web.'

'Oh, hurry!' said Wilbur. 'Hurry up, Templeton!'

But the rat was in no hurry…

Wilbur was desperate. The people were coming. And the rat was failing him. Suddenly he remembered Templeton's fondness for food.

'Templeton,' he said, 'I will make you a solemn promise. Get Charlotte's egg sac for me, and from now on… I will let you have your choice of everything in the trough and I won't touch a thing until you're through.'

The rat sat up. 'You mean that?' he said.

'I promise. I cross my heart.'

'All right, it's a deal,' said the rat. He walked to the wall and started to climb… Wilbur watched from below.

'Use extreme care!' he said. 'I don't want a single one of those eggs harmed.'

'Thith thtuff thticks in my mouth,' complained the rat. 'It'th worth than caramel candy.'

But Templeton worked away at the job, and managed to cut the sac adrift and carry it to the ground, where he dropped it in front of Wilbur. Wilbur heaved a great sigh of relief.

'Thank you, Templeton,' he said. 'I will never forget this as long as I live.'...

Wilbur had already decided how he would carry the egg sac – there was only one way possible. He carefully took the little bundle in his mouth and held it there on top of his tongue. He remembered what Charlotte had told him – that the sac was waterproof and strong. It felt funny on his tongue and made him drool a bit. And of course he couldn't say anything. But as he was being shoved into the crate, he looked up at Charlotte and gave her a wink. She knew he was saying good-bye in the only way he could. And she knew her children were safe.

'Good-bye!' she whispered. Then she summoned all her strength and waved one of her front legs at him.

She never moved again. Next day, as the Ferris wheel was being taken apart and the race horses were being loaded into vans and the entertainers were packing up their belongings and driving away in their trailers, Charlotte died.

And so Wilbur came home to his beloved manure pile in the barn cellar. His was a strange home-coming. Around his neck he wore a medal of honour; in his mouth he held a sac of spider's eggs. There is no place like home, Wilbur thought, as he placed Charlotte's five hundred and fourteen unborn children carefully in a safe corner. The barn smelled good. His friends the sheep and the geese were glad to see him back.

The geese gave him a noisy welcome.

'Congratu-congratu-congratulations!' they cried. 'Nice work.'

Mr Zuckerman took the medal from Wilbur's neck and hung it on a nail over the pigpen, where visitors could examine it. Wilbur himself could look at it whenever he wanted to.

In the days that followed, he was very happy. He grew to a great size. He no longer worried about being killed, for he knew that Mr Zuckerman would keep him as long as he lived. Wilbur often thought of Charlotte. A few strands of her old web still hung in the doorway. Every day Wilbur would stand and look at the torn, empty web, and a lump would come to his throat. No one had ever been such a friend – so affectionate, so loyal, and so skilful.

The autumn days grew shorter...

All winter Wilbur watched over Charlotte's egg sac as though he were guarding his own children. He had scooped out a special place in the manure for the sac, next to the board fence. On very cold nights he lay so that his breath would warm it. For Wilbur, nothing in life was so important as this small round object – nothing else mattered. Patiently he awaited the end of the winter and the coming of the little spiders. Life is always a rich and steady time when you are waiting for something to happen or to hatch. The winter ended at last.

'I heard the frogs today,' said the old sheep one evening. 'Listen! You can hear them now.'

Wilbur stood still and cocked his ears. From the pond, in shrill chorus, came the voices of hundreds of little frogs.

'Springtime,' said the old sheep, thoughtfully. 'Another spring.' As she walked away, Wilbur saw a new lamb following her. It was only a few hours old...

One fine sunny morning, after breakfast, Wilbur stood watching his precious sac. He wasn't thinking of anything much. As he stood there, he noticed something move. He stepped closer and stared. A tiny spider crawled from the sac. It was no bigger than a grain of sand, no bigger than the head of a pin. Its body was grey with a black stripe underneath. Its legs were grey and tan. It looked just like Charlotte.

Wilbur trembled all over when he saw it. The little spider waved at him. Then Wilbur looked more closely. Two more little spiders crawled out and waved. They climbed round and round on the sac, exploring their new world. Then three more little spiders. Then eight. Then ten. Charlotte's children were here at last.

Wilbur's heart pounded. He began to squeal. Then he raced in circles, kicking manure into the air. Then he turned a back flip. Then he planted his front feet and came to a stop in front of Charlotte's children.

'Hello there!' he said.

The first spider said hello, but its voice was so small Wilbur couldn't hear it.

'I am an old friend of your mother's,' said Wilbur. 'I'm glad to see you.'

'Transplant'*

ARWEN CLAYDON (AGED 11)

In death we find life,
In sorrow joy.
The ending of a song and beginning of another,
New life arising from the ashes of old life,
A dark cold winter means a fresh green spring –
Sadness brings new hope,
Thus sorrow and joy meet and become one.

* This poem was inspired by a television report of a successful organ transplant.

A Goose Called Gloria

JEAN WATSON

Dreamy goose Gloria lived on a farm with lots of other geese. The farmer and his wife were called Mr and Mrs Mackay. Most farmers clipped the wings of their geese to stop them flying away. But Mr Mackay didn't always bother.

'Och! Our geese won't fly away. They have everything they need right here,' he said.

'Aye, they do so,' his wife agreed.

Every day she came into the farmyard to feed the geese.

'Come away, now!' she called, scattering wheat and grits all around her.

As soon as they heard her calling, the geese came running. They picked up the food from the ground in their strong beaks, then swallowed it all the way down their long, long necks. If they were still hungry, they could waddle off the meadow to graze on the grass.

When they were thirsty, they had cool, clean water to drink. When they were hot, they wandered down to the pond for a splash or a swim.

Sometimes it rained. Sometimes it snowed. Then the farmer and his wife covered the ground with straw, so the geese could keep their feet dry. At night, they slept, warm and dry, on bales of hay in their own little wooden houses.

By day and by night they were kept safe, for all around the farm were tall fences which kept away hungry foxes.

The geese were happy. 'We've got it made!' they gloated. 'Everything we need! No enemies to fear or fight! No work to do, except lay our eggs!' Of course, they grew fatter and fatter and slept a lot. But that didn't worry them.

It worried Gloria, though. She had the strangest feeling that they were missing something. Something that really mattered. And then one day a flock of wild geese flew over the farmyard.

Hearing their honking cries, the farmyard geese lifted their

long, long necks and watched them. But as soon as the wild birds could be heard and seen no more, the farmyard geese lowered their heads and forgot all about them.

All except Gloria.

'Where are they going?' she asked.

'Over mountains and across oceans, following the sun,' said fat goose Fred. 'It makes me tired just thinking about it.'

'It doesn't make me tired,' said Gloria. 'It makes me tingle all over.'

'Sounds to me like a bad attack of goose-pimples,' said funny goose Jo.

But Gloria said, 'I wish I was up there with them.'

'Don't be a silly goose,' said Jo. 'They're wild and we're tame.'

'But we've all got wings,' said Gloria. 'And what are wings for if not for flying?'

Just then Mrs Mackay the farmer's wife came into the farmyard.

'Come away, now!' she called, scattering wheat and grits all around her.

As soon as they heard her calling, the geese came running. They picked up their food from the ground in their strong beaks, then swallowed it all the way down their long, long necks.

But afterwards, when the other geese went to sleep, Gloria wandered round the farm, asking questions about the wild geese and about what lay beyond the farmyard.

But the cows and horses swatted her with their tails. 'You're more bothersome than a hundred flies,' they said.

And the goat waved his horns at her. 'You're harder to get rid of than goose-grass,' he said between mouthfuls.

And the dog snarled at her. 'Ack-ack-ack! Your voice is worse than a yowling cat's,' he said.

And when the other geese woke up and heard what had happened, they weren't very pleased with her either.

'Stop being a gooseberry fool!' said Jo.

'Life here is easy. Make the most of it,' said Fred.

Gloria did try, but it wasn't any use. Because now she knew they were missing something. Something that really mattered.

She tried to tell the other geese about it, but they weren't interested. So Gloria had to go it alone. It was scary, but she'd made up her mind.

One night, when everyone else was asleep, Gloria crept out of doors and went on her first do-it-yourself flying lesson. She flew as high and as far as she could. It wasn't very high or very far, but it was a start. And the next night she did a little better. And the night after that, she did better still.

After weeks of practice, she could fly up, up, up, as high as she liked, or dive down, down, down as low as she pleased. And she could hover on currents of air for as long as she wanted to, or zoom to and fro as fast as she chose.

Now she was ready – and only just in time. For the very next day a flock of wild geese flew over the farmyard.

Hearing their honking cries, the farmyard geese lifted their long, long necks and watched them.

All except Gloria.

She flew up, up, up into the sky calling, 'Goodbye. I'll come back and tell you all about it one day.' The words grew fainter and fainter, the higher she flew.

Mr and Mrs Mackay came out of the farmhouse just in time to see a lone goose flying straight up into the air towards a flock of wild geese.

'Och! That's never one of ours,' said Mr Mackay. 'Our geese wouldn't fly away. They have everything they need right here.'

'Aye, they do so,' his wife agreed. Then he went off to see to the other farm animals and she got on with feeding the geese.

'Come away, now!' she called, scattering wheat and grits all around her.

As soon as they heard her calling, the geese lowered their heads and came running. They picked up the food from the ground in their strong beaks, then swallowed it all the way down their long,

long necks. And they forgot all about Gloria and the wild geese and got on with their easy, farmyard lives.

But Gloria didn't forget her friends or her promise. And one day she came swooping down from the sky and made a perfect landing in the middle of the farmyard.

'It's me, Gloria! I'm back, but not for long,' she said as the farmyard geese gathered round or looked up from their picking and pecking. 'I came on ahead, because I just had to come and tell you how wonderful it is to fly, fly, fly, high over the mountains and the oceans, following the sun.'

'But is it safe?' asked funny goose Jo.

'And is it easy?' asked fat goose Fred.

'Oh no!' laughed Gloria. 'It can be hard and dangerous. No one brings us food – we have to find it for ourselves. Sometimes we fly into storms. Sometimes we are attacked by bigger birds. On the ground, there may be foxes and other enemies. But as we struggle, we learn and grow stronger. And there's nothing more exciting and brilliant than flying! Riding on the winds, exploring the sky, making our home in new places, then, when the seasons change, moving on again. That's the life we were born, born, born for! Why don't you come and join us? Think about it. Dream about it. You'll find a way if you really want to, just as I did. But now I must go, for I can hear a distant honking, which means that the rest of the flock will soon be overhead. Goodbyeeeeeeee!'

The farmyard geese watched and listened until Gloria and the wild geese could be heard and seen no more. Then they lowered their heads and forgot all about them.

All except a gander called Goldie.

'Where are they going?' he asked...

'Faith and Doubt'

ANON

Doubt sees the obstacles,
Faith sees the way;
Doubt sees the blackest night,
Faith sees the day;

Doubt dreads to take a step,
Faith soars on high;
Doubt questions, 'Who believes?'
Faith answers, 'I!'

The Tale of Geronimo Grub

Based on Mrs Gatty's *Parables From Nature*

RETOLD BY PAT WYNNEJONES

The village pond was shimmering in the spring sunshine. Bulrushes and forget-me-nots fringed its sides, perfectly reflected in the shining surface.

Below that surface there was a wonderful underwater kingdom, dark and mysterious, where Geronimo the grub and his brothers searched for their food and played hide-and-seek, darting in and out of the shadows and shafts of sunlight among the water plants.

Geronimo was inquisitive. He was curious about the world he lived in, for ever wondering why and asking questions.

'Don't be so nosey!' his brothers would tease.

'I wonder where the old Frog goes to,' Geronimo pondered one day. 'He swims upward to the top of the pond and he disappears from sight – till – plop! There he is again when we least expect him.'

'Who cares where the old Frog goes?' laughed Gerald.

'Let's just look out for our own food,' agreed George, 'and leave other people's business alone.'

'But do you think he leaves this world?' persisted Geronimo. 'Do you think there can be something – somewhere – beyond?'

'Why don't you ask him yourself?' suggested a young minnow, with a mischievous twinkle in his eye. For the Frog was a dignified person who might well consider the questions impertinent. But at last Geronimo screwed up his courage.

'Respected Frog, sir,' he began politely, 'if you please, sir, there is something I would like to ask you.'

'I don't please,' replied the Frog, in a not very encouraging tone, and looking at the little grub with obvious annoyance. 'But ask away, ask away, if you must.'

'Well, sir,' Geronimo began very shyly, 'can you please tell me what there is beyond this world?'

'What world do you mean, little grub?'

'This world of ours – our world – I mean, respected Frog, sir.'

'This little tiny pond, I suppose you mean,' replied the Frog scornfully. 'Well, I'll tell you. There is dry land. Dry land with beautiful green grass and meadows filled with golden buttercups and sweet white daisies; and there are huge stately trees and blue skies and dreamy white clouds and brilliant sunshine.'

'Wow!' exclaimed Geronimo, but he did not believe it. For he knew only the dark waters of the pond.

'Dry land?' he repeated wonderingly. 'Can you swim about in it?'

'Of course not!' chuckled the Frog. 'Dry land is not water, my little fellow – that is just what it is *not*!' And he blew some bubbles to show his amusement.

'Well,' Geronimo persisted, feeling rather put down. 'What *is* it then?'

'You really are the most inquisitive creature I have ever come across. Well, dry land is rather like the sludge at the bottom of this pond, only it is not wet because there is no water.'

'What is there, then?'

'Oh, there is air and sunshine and light...'

'What is *air*, respected Frog, sir?'

But this was the last straw as far as the Frog was concerned, for he really was exasperated by all the questions.

'Since you're so eager to find out what lies above, I'll give you a ride up on my back and you can see for yourself,' he offered.

Geronimo was delighted. He climbed onto the Frog's back and up they went – up and up and up!

But the moment they reached the surface – crash! He reeled back into the pond as though he had hit an invisible wall, gasping and panting for breath. He could not live in the air. He belonged to the life of the pond.

He clung to the stem of a water plant, trembling with shock and disappointment, until the Frog swam down and joined him.

'There is nothing beyond this pond but death,' he wept. 'Nothing but death. Why did you tell me all those stories about beautiful colours and flowers and bright light? About another world beyond?'

The Frog regarded him severely. 'I told you those "stories", as you call them,' he said sternly, 'because they are true. But because you know only this little pond you will not believe there is anything beyond it.'

He swam away and Geronimo did not see him for a few days. Then he came looking for the dragonfly grub with important news.

'Quick, quick – here!' he called. 'I've something to tell you. I've just seen something strange – something that should interest you. I saw a grub like you climbing up the stalk of a bulrush until he was *right out* of the water, in the full glare of the sun. Then as I watched there came a rent in his skin and with many struggles there emerged one of those radiant creatures that dazzle the eyes – a glorious dragonfly!'

Geronimo listened in amazement. He could not believe it!

'Was this beautiful creature really once a grub like me?'

As the spring days grew warmer Geronimo began to feel strange. His eyes became large and brilliant, and some extraordinary force seemed to be urging him upwards, upwards! He began struggling slowly up a bulrush stem towards the surface.

His brothers gather round anxiously, begging him not to go.

'Don't leave us!' they cried pitifully.

'I cannot help it,' he gasped. 'Go I must.'

'Then promise you will come back and tell us what lies beyond,' Gerald implored.

'Don't forget us,' entreated George.

'Never!' Geronimo answered firmly. 'I will never forget you. I promise to return and tell you what I have seen.'

And then he was gone. He had disappeared as completely as the Frog had done. For Gerald and George could not perceive anything beyond the pond.

They waited patiently for hours, and then for days, but he never came back. At last they gave up hope of ever seeing him again.

'He has forgotten us,' said Gerald bitterly.

But had Geronimo forgotten his brothers? No indeed! The Frog had been right. He had left his grub body when he left the pond. He had become a glorious dragonfly, and risen with glittering wings into the sunshine. He had not forgotten his brothers, but he could not return to them.

He could fly over the green meadow with its stately trees, its golden buttercups and sweet white daisies. He could soar into the blue skies.

But he did not forget those he had loved and had left in the dark pond waters. Though they did not know it, gleams like star-rays were dropping from his gorgeous wings into the shadows of their world.

But try as he would Geronimo could not return to them. The pond surface was like a wall to him. Just as he could not pass through it from below when he was a pond creature, so he could not penetrate it from above once he had become a creature of the air.

So he hovered above, waiting for his brothers to climb the bulrush stems and become dragonflies like him. He was there, hovering on radiant wings to welcome, first Gerald, then George, into the breezy air.

They had never hoped to see one another again, but oh! what joy now they were re-united. They darted to and fro, their brilliant green and blue wings flashing fire, in the ecstasy of their new life together.

'Morning Has Broken'

ELEANOR FARJEON

Morning has broken like the first morning.
Blackbird has spoken like the first bird.
Praise for the singing! Praise for the morning!
Praise for them springing fresh from the word.

Sweet the rain's new fall, sunlit from heaven,
Like the first dewfall on the first grass.
Praise for the sweetness of the wet garden,
Sprung in completeness where His feet pass.

Mine is the sunlight, mine is the morning.
Born of the one light Eden saw play.
Praise with elation, praise every morning,
God's recreation of the new day.

Acknowledgments

Thanks go to all those who have given permission to include material in this book, as indicated in the list below. Every effort has been made to trace and contact copyright owners. We apologize for any inadvertent omissions or errors.

Extracts from *The Lion Children's Bible* by Pat Alexander, published by Lion Publishing plc. 'The Best Easter Present Ever' by Sue Atkinson, copyright © 1997. 'Entering In' copyright © Jean Barker. 'The Greatest Love' from *The Everyday Book* by Mary Batchelor, copyright © 1982. 'Hands' by Clare Brooks, copyright © Turning Heads. 'The Donkey' by G.K. Chesterton, by permission of A.P. Watt Ltd on behalf of the Royal Literary Fund. 'Transplant' by Arwen Claydon, copyright © Turning Heads. 'Quarrel' by Jeremy Consitt, copyright © Turning Heads. 'Love is Come Again' from 'Now the green blade riseth' by J.M. Crum, from the *Oxford Book of Carols*. 'Consolation Prize' by Lavinia Derwent copyright © by the Estate of Lavinia Derwent. Reprinted by permission of Mary Baxter. 'There is a smudge of bad in all of us' by Michael Duggan, copyright © Turning Heads. Text of *The Tale of Three Trees* by Angela Elwell Hunt, published by Lion Publishing plc. 'Morning has Broken' by Eleanor Farjeon, from *The Children's Bells*, published by Oxford University Press. 'The Soldier Who Took the Blame' from *Miracle on the River Kwai* by Ernest Gordon, published by HarperCollins Publishers Ltd. 'Paradise Hill' from *The Little White Horse* by Elizabeth Goudge, published by Lion Publishing plc. 'Excitement at Easter' and 'Easter' by Wendy Green, copyright © 1997. 'That's It!' from *Child of the Covenant*, copyright © 1985 by Michele Guinness. Reproduced by permission of Hodder & Stoughton. 'Angel of Death and Life' from *Angels, Angels All Around* by Bob Hartman, published by Lion Publishing US, a division of Chariot Victor Publishing, copyright © 1992. Extracts from *The Lion Storyteller Bible* by Bob Hartman, published by Lion Publishing plc. 'A Life for a Life' by Peggy Hewitt, copyright © 1997. 'On Easter Day' from *In the Springtime of the Year*, published by Penguin Books, copyright © Susan Hill, 1974, 1989. All rights reserved. 'The Friends' from *I am David* by Anne Holm, published by Methuen Children's Books. Reprinted by permission of Reed Consumer Books. 'Winners' by Nan Hunt, copyright © 1997. 'The Interview' from *The Davidson Affair* by Stuart Jackman, published by Faber and Faber Ltd. 'The Founding of Narnia' from *The Magician's Nephew* by C.S. Lewis, published by HarperCollins Publishers Ltd. 'The White Witch', 'The Death of Aslan' and 'Deeper Magic' from *The Lion, the Witch and the Wardrobe* by C.S. Lewis, published by HarperCollins Publishers Ltd. 'Good Friday's Bad!' and 'Pieces of Howl' from *Haffertee's First Christmas*, published by Lion Publishing plc, copyright © 1977 Janet and John Perkins. Text of *The Donkey's Day Out*, published by Lion Publishing plc, copyright © 1990 Ann Pilling. 'The Pelican' by Ann Pilling, reprinted by permission of Reed Consumer Books. 'Stefan's Prisoner' from *Dark Journey* by Jenny Robertson, copyright © Scripture Union, used by permission. 'The Colour of Easter', 'Real Forgiveness' and 'The Easter Worm' copyright © Coral Rumble. 'The Oak Tree' by Fay Sampson, copyright © 1997. 'The Slave-Girl and the King', 'Ring a Ring o' Roses', and 'Elleni and the Sharing Bread' copyright © Arthur Scholey. 'Love Your Enemy' from *Tramp for the Lord* by Corrie ten Boom. Reprinted with permission from Guideposts Magazine. Copyright © 1972 by Guideposts, Carmel, NY 10512, USA. 'In the Beginning' copyright © Steve Turner from *The Day I Fell Down the Toilet and Other Poems*, published by Lion Publishing plc. 'The Easter Egg' from *The Country Child* by Alison Uttley, published by Faber and Faber Ltd. 'A Light in the Dark' from *The Manger is Empty*, copyright © 1989 by Walter Wangerin, Jr. Reprinted by permission of HarperCollins Publishers, Inc. 'Simeon's Donkey' by Eleanor Watkins, copyright © 1997. Text of *The Day the Robbers Came* and 'A Goose Called Gloria' copyright © Jean Watson. 'Charlotte's Day' from *Charlotte's Web* by E.B. White (Hamish Hamilton Children's Books, 1952), copyright © 1952 by J. White. 'The Tale of Geronimo Grub' copyright © Pat Wynnejones.